新时代行业英语系列教材

U0361697

总主编 姜 宏

主 编 冯茂芳

副主编 杨明军 李泓桥

编 者 刘 莉 李 梅 张严心

原版作者 Alison Smith

市场营销与广告英语

ENGLISH for

Marketing & Advertising

清华大学出版社

北京

北京市版权局著作权合同登记号　图字：01-2021-1540

图书在版编目（CIP）数据

市场营销与广告英语 / 姜宏总主编；冯茂芳主编. —北京：清华大学出版社，2021.4
新时代行业英语系列教材
ISBN 978-7-302-57791-1

Ⅰ.①市… Ⅱ.①姜… ②冯… Ⅲ.①市场营销–英语–高等职业教育–教材②广告–英语–高等职业教育–教材
Ⅳ.①F713.3②F713.8

中国版本图书馆 CIP 数据核字（2021）第 055435 号

策划编辑：刘细珍
责任编辑：刘　艳
封面设计：子　一
责任校对：王凤芝
责任印制：丛怀宇

出版发行：清华大学出版社
　　　　　　网　　址：http://www.tup.com.cn, http://www.wqbook.com
　　　　　　地　　址：北京清华大学学研大厦 A 座　　邮　编：100084
　　　　　　社 总 机：010-62770175　　　　　　邮　购：010-62786544
　　　　　　投稿与读者服务：010-62776969, c-service@tup.tsinghua.edu.cn
　　　　　　质 量 反 馈：010-62772015, zhiliang@tup.tsinghua.edu.cn
印 装 者：北京博海升彩色印刷有限公司
经　　销：全国新华书店
开　　本：210mm×285mm　　**印　张**：9.75　　　**字　数**：236 千字
版　　次：2021 年 4 月第 1 版　　　　　　　　**印　次**：2021 年 4 月第 1 次印刷
定　　价：55.00 元

产品编号：091259-01

在经济全球化和国际交往日益频繁的今天，无论是作为个人还是组织的一员，参与国际交流与合作都需要具备良好的外语沟通能力和扎实的专业技术能力。高职院校承担着培养具有全球竞争力的高端技术技能人才的使命，需要探索如何有效地培养学生的行业外语能力。行业外语教学一直是职业院校的短板，缺少合适的教材是其中一个主要原因。目前，国内大多数高职院校在第一学年开设公共英语课程，所用教材多为通用英语教材，其主题与学生所学专业的关联度总体较低；部分院校自主开发的行业英语教材，在专业内容的系统性、语言表达的准确性等方面存在诸多不足；还有部分院校直接采用国外原版的大学本科或研究生教材，但这些教材学术性和专业性太强，对以就业为导向的高职院校学生来说，十分晦涩难懂。

清华大学出版社从欧洲引进原版素材并组织国内一线行业英语教师改编的这套"新时代行业英语系列教材"，以提升学生职业英语能力为目标，服务师生教与学。本套教材体现了如下特点：

一、编写理念突出全球化和国际化

本套教材引进欧洲原版优质资源，全球化视角选材，结合行业领域和单元主题，关注环境保护、人口老龄化、贫困等时代难题，培养学生的国际视野和世界公民素养。单元主题、板块编排和练习设计与国际接轨，体现国际规范和国际标准，且反映全球行业发展动态和前景，帮助学生全面了解全球行业现状和掌握国际操作流程，夯实行业知识体系。

二、编写目标注重培养学生使用英语完成工作任务的实际应用能力

为响应高职院校外语教学改革号召，培养具有国际竞争力的高端技术技能人才，将外语教学目标由原来的语言能力导向转变为职业能力导向，本套教材通过听、说、读、写、译等基本语言技能训练，让学生完成不同行业领域的工作任务，将英语放到职场的背景中来学，放到员工的岗位职责、工作流程中来学。

三、结构与内容紧扣行业领域的职场情境和核心业务

本套教材围绕行业核心概念和业务组织教学单元，不同单元相互关联，内容由浅入深、由易到难，循序渐进；教材各单元主题契合行业典型工作场景，内容反映职业岗位核心业务知识与流程。每本教材根据内容设置 8 至 10 个单元，用多种形式的语言训练任务提升学生对行业知识的理解与应用。

四、资源立体多样，方便师生教与学

本套教材图文并茂。通过改编，在原版教材基础上每个单元增加了学习目标，明确了学生在完成各单元学习后应该达到的知识和能力水平；增加了重点词汇中文注释和专业术语表，便于学生准确理解行业核心概念；听力练习和阅读篇章均配有音频，并借助二维码扫码听音的形式呈现，实现教材的立体化，方便学生学习；习题安排契合单元的主题内容，便于检测单元学习目标的实现程度。教材另配有电子课件和习题答案，方便教师备课与授课。教师可以征订教材后联系出版社索取。

本套教材共10本，包括《护理英语》《机电英语》《建筑工程英语》《运输与物流英语》《烹饪、餐饮与接待英语》《旅游英语》《银行与金融英语》《市场营销与广告英语》《商务英语》《商务会谈英语》，涵盖医药卫生、机电设备、土木建筑、交通运输、旅游、财经商贸等六大类专业。建议高职院校结合本校人才培养目标，开设相应课程。

本套教材适合作为高职院校学生的行业英语教材，也适合相关行业从业人员作为培训或自学教材。

姜宏

2021年3月31日

前言

　　《市场营销与广告英语》是为高职学生打造的一本行业英语教材。编写团队结合中国学生的实际英语水平，本着培养学生职业能力、助力学生职业发展的原则，对原版引进教材的内容进行了整合、删减，最大程度保留了原版教材的特色，并增加了相应的符合中国国情的具体内容。本书包括10个单元，内容分别是：营销步骤及营销组合，SWOT分析，市场调研及数据分析，主动优惠，促销信函，广告的目的及历史，广告媒体，产品植入、赞助及贸易展览会，广告分析，求职，供市场营销专业或商科相关专业高职学生一学期使用。本书改编后具有以下特色：

　　1. 每个单元的首页都明确提出了学习目标。学习目标具体、实用，具有操作性，学生学习时能够做到心中有数、有的放矢。

　　2. 每个单元开始学习前，都有一个简短的Starting Off，旨在引出话题、增加知识点，让学生熟悉本单元的主题，顺利过渡到本单元内容的学习。

　　3. 每个单元都设计了丰富多样的练习题型，以"微"活动实践和"微"知识点来激发学生的学习兴趣。这样的设计便于教师灵活指导，提升课堂教学效果。本书始终秉承"教、学、做"为一体的精神，注重培养学生的思考能力、合作能力、探究能力、动手能力，为学生积极思考和创新实践创造条件。学生在提高语言基本技能的同时，也巩固和拓宽了专业知识。

　　4. 每个单元都补充了富有时代气息的鲜活营销案例或相关的知识，让学生对所学的内容有所思考，同时也增加了本书的丰富性、实用性、趣味性。

　　5. 在词汇的学习上，每个单元除了基本的生词外，还专门列出了本单元的实用表达及专业词汇，加强学生对专业词汇的掌握。

　　本书的主编冯茂芳改编了第1、2、3、4、5、6、10单元，副主编杨明军改编了第8和第9单元，副主编李泓桥改编了第7单元；编者刘莉、李梅、张严心为本书的资料收集和审核做了部分辅助工作；另外，姜宏院长为本书的改编提出了许多宝贵的意见。在此对所有参编人员表示感谢。

编者

2021年3月

Contents

Learning Objectives

Upon completion of the unit, students will be able to:

- define marketing and explain the 4 Ps, 4 Cs and the extended 3 Ps;
- apply the 4 Ps, 4 Cs and the extended 3 Ps to market a product;
- write an essay on one of the 4 Ps of marketing mix;
- have professional abilities and good communication skills in marketing.

Starting Off

Marketing is a form of commercial activity, widely used by individuals and institutions to create awareness and build an image of their products/services, in the minds of potential buyers. The American Marketing Association defines marketing as "the activity, set of institutions, and processes for creating, communicating, delivering, and exchanging offerings that have value for customers, clients, partners, and society at large". Blog marketing, social media marketing, email marketing and other online avenues such as search engine marketing (SEO and PPC) are common marketing approaches. Whether it is a physical business, or an online business, it is important for marketers to integrate their offline marketing with online marketing and use a multiple channels system to promote their products/services. Let's go on and explore more.

Reading 1

Marketing starts with the customers: They should be at the centre of any business activity. Through marketing a company can **identify** and **analyse** the needs of its customers and then make the relevant decisions in order to **satisfy** these needs, promote them and make a profit. This means marketing **comprises** the following steps:

Identifying

This **involves** answering questions such as "How do we find out what the consumer's **requirements** are?" and "How do we keep in touch with their thoughts and feelings and **perceptions** about our goods or service?". This is fundamental to market research.

Anticipating

Consumer requirements are constantly changing. Anticipation involves looking ahead to guess how those changes will **alter** customers' needs. Marketers also need to try to **anticipate** what Next Best Thing (NBT) customers will be wanting, whether it is a particular service or new **feature** of a product.

Satisfying

The marketing process has to be pleasing to consumers in order to **convince** them that the product will satisfy their needs or wants. In this way, they will be persuaded to **purchase** or use that particular product or service.

Profitability

Marketing has to be **balanced** in order for a business to make a profit and continue to **operate**. A marketing **budget** must be **sufficient** in order to function correctly and achieve the desired results, but care must be taken not to **overspend** and reduce **overall** profits for the company.

MY GLOSSARY

identify	v.	确认；找到，发现
analyse	v.	分析，解析
satisfy	v.	满足；令人满意
comprise	v.	包括，包含；由……组成
involve	v.	包含；需要
requirement	n.	需求；必需品
perception	n.	感知，感觉
alter	v.	改变
anticipate	v.	预料；预期；预计
feature	n.	特色，特征

convince	v.	使确信，使相信，使信服
purchase	v.	购买；获得
profitability	n.	盈利能力；收益性；利益率
balance	v.	保持平衡；使相等
operate	v.	运转；工作
budget	n.	预算；财政收支状况
sufficient	adj.	足够的，充足的
overspend	v.	超支；花钱过多
overall	adj.	总体的；全面的；综合的

1 Read the text and answer these questions.

1) Who is at the centre of marketing activities?

_____

2) Why do businesses practise marketing?

_____

3) What is the key purpose of market research?

_____

4) What does the acronym NBT stand for and what purpose does it serve for marketers?

_____

5) Why is customer satisfaction important?

_____

6) Why is it important for a company to stay within its marketing budget?

_____

2 Marketing uses a lot of acronyms. Here are some common acronyms for describing demographic groups. Match each one to the correct definition.

1) DINKY	a ☐	two incomes, nanny and kids
2) YOOFS	b ☐	a green young urban professional
3) YUPPIE	c ☐	young, free and single
4) NILKIE	d ☐	older people with active lifestyles
5) TINKIE	e ☐	double income, no kids yet
6) GUPPIE	f ☐	greying, leisured, affluent, middle-aged
7) OPAL	g ☐	no income, lots of kids
8) GLAM	h ☐	young, urban professional

3 Translate the following expressions into Chinese.

1) market research _____

2) marketing process _____

3) marketing budget _____

4) make a profit _____

5) satisfy one's needs _____

6) consumer's requirements _____

7) achieve the desired results _____

8) overall profits _____

4 Fill in the blanks with the words from the box, changing the form if necessary.

profit	anticipate	identify	promote
purchase	profitability	satisfy	analyse

1) _____ that sales will fall, the company gave third quarter guidance.

2) The company made a healthy _____ on the deal.

3) The area is being _____ as a tourist destination.

4) Even the biggest victims of the crisis expect to return to _____ this year.

5) Internet digital technology is _____ the needs of individuals to acquire information.

6) She is prepared to offer me an amount adequate to _____ another house.

7) Managers _____ their company's data and compare it with data on their competitors.

8) As yet they have not _____ a buyer for the company.

Speaking 1

5 **What do you think the purpose of marketing is? How important is it for a company? Talk together.**

Reading 2

Four main factors, commonly known as the 4 Ps, determine how a product will be marketed. These elements—product, price, place and **promotion**—can be adjusted to find the right **combination** that will appeal to the customer and **simultaneously** serve his or her needs while generating **optimum** profits.

Product

The perfect product must provide value for the customer and give customers what they want, not what producers think they want. It also needs to look good, work well and be different from **competitors'** products, for example in the quality, size, design, **packaging**, etc.

 Price

Since price is the only element in the marketing mix that generates a **revenue**, pricing must be **calculated** to provide a profit. One pricing strategy is "cost-plus pricing" which is when the cost of production, **distribution** and other **overheads** are calculated and then a profit **mark-up** is added. Other strategies take into consideration what potential customers are prepared to pay for the product or the price that competitors' products are sold at.

Place

A product must reach the right place, at the right time and in the right **quantity** for customers so it is vital for a company to choose the correct distribution channel for its products. Market and product factors, such as buyer behaviour and the type of product, as well as **aspects** like the size of the business and costs, will **influence** this choice.

Promotion

sale

Promotion is the way a company provides customers with information about itself and its products. It includes activities like branding, advertising, public relations, special offers, exhibitions, etc. Promotion is important to improve a company's image, launch a new product, increase **popularity** of existing products, attract new customers and, naturally, increase sales.

MY GLOSSARY

promotion	n.	促销活动; 广告宣传; 推广	distribution	n.	分销; 分布; 分配
combination	n.	结合; 联合; 混合	overheads	n.	企业的一般管理费用; 日常开支
simultaneously	adv.	同时地			
optimum	adj.	最佳的; 最适宜的	mark-up	n.	涨价; 加于成本之价格
competitor	n.	竞争者; 对手	quantity	n.	数量
packaging	n.	包装材料; 外包装	aspect	n.	方面; 层面
revenue	n.	收益; 税收收入	influence	v.	影响; 作用
calculate	v.	计算; 核算	popularity	n.	普及; 流行; 受欢迎

6 **Read the text and decide if these sentences are true (*T*) or false (*F*). If there is not enough information, choose "doesn't say" (*DS*).**

		T	F	DS
1)	The correct mix of the 4 Ps is essential to market a product successfully.	☐	☐	☐
2)	The perfect product should meet customers' requirements.	☐	☐	☐
3)	Pricing strategies never generate profits for a company.	☐	☐	☐
4)	A company should always price its product lower than a competitor's.	☐	☐	☐
5)	It is important to consider the type of product when choosing a distribution channel.	☐	☐	☐
6)	Promotion is not necessary for existing products but only for new ones.	☐	☐	☐

7 Match each word to its meaning.

1) optimum	a ☐	the act of mixing two or more things to form a single unit
2) combination	b ☐	the best possible
3) packaging	c ☐	the standard of something
4) revenue	d ☐	the activity of giving a particular name and image to goods and services
5) overheads	e ☐	regular costs that you have when you are running a business
6) branding	f ☐	the money that an organisation, etc. receives from its business
7) exhibition	g ☐	the act of showing something to the public
8) quality	h ☐	the process of wrapping goods

Speaking 2

8 Discuss these questions in small groups.

1) Why do you choose one particular brand over another?
2) Is there a product you usually buy? What is it?
3) What product would you never buy? Why?
4) What would convince you to buy it?

Listening

9 First try to complete the following conversation, and then listen to the recording to check your answers.

M: Hi Mary. What do you think the purpose of marketing is?

W: Well, through marketing a company can (1)_____.

M: What does a company do in order to generate optimum profits?

W: Marketing comprises the following steps: identifying, anticipating, (2)_____ and profitability.

M: Oh, a company has to identify and analyse the needs of its customers and then make the relevant decisions in order to satisfy these needs, (3)_____ them and make a profit.

W: Of course. Do you know four main factors, commonly known as the 4 Ps?

M: Yes, they determine how products will be (4)_____. These elements include product, price, (5)_____ and promotion.

W: What are the most important things in a marketing mix?

M: It should be the right combination that will (6)_____ the customer and simultaneously (7)_____ his or her needs.

W: I always choose one particular brand because of their promotion activities.

M: Promotion is important to attract new and old customers, which will naturally (8)_____.

Writing

10 **Choose one of the 4 Ps. Describe its importance and how it is used to market a product with your examples.**

Reading 3

The 4 Cs

The 4 Cs is a more consumer-oriented model of the marketing mix, taking into consideration the customer's point of view. The four factors are consumer, cost, communication and **convenience** which focus on what consumers want or need, the costs they **incur**, all the **interactions** with them and how and where they prefer to purchase the product or service. The 4 Cs can be considered an important part of **relationship** or **relational** marketing, the current trend where marketing strategy focuses on **establishing** a long-term relationship with customers instead of just **concluding** the sale, which is the goal of **transactional** marketing.

MY GLOSSARY

convenience	*n.*	便利; 便利的事物		relational	*adj.*	有关的, 相关的
incur	*v.*	引致, 带来（成本、花费等）		establish	*v.*	建立; 确立
interaction	*n.*	相互作用; 相互影响		conclude	*v.*	（使）结束, 终止
relationship	*n.*	关系; 联系		transactional	*adj.*	交易型的; 事务性的

11 **Read the text and answer these questions.**

1) What does the 4 Cs model take into consideration?

_____

2) What does the factor "communication" refer to?

_____

3) What does the factor "convenience" refer to?

_____

4) What is the difference between relational marketing and transactional marketing?

_____

12 **Complete the following sentences with the words from this unit. Some letters have been given.**

1) The firm is working on a new product in com_____ with several overseas partners.

2) The analysis was applied to each scenario to determine the op_____ scope of the services.

3) If your com_____ has a coffee shop with a wide array of beverages and food items, narrow it down: Offer just one kind of coffee, but make it amazing.

4) The oldest Disney theme park receives over 14 million visitors each year, nearly $3 billion in re_____.

5) Expectation management can help sales professionals understand the organisation, relationships and motivations of a po_____ customer.

6) Which turns out to be a fairly good business, with over_____ low enough to make a reasonable profit?

7) Price is determined through the in_____ of demand and supply.

8) For (the sake of) con_____, the two groups have been treated as one in this report.

Reading 4

The Extended Marketing Mix

Nowadays, it is common to add three extra Ps to the traditional marketing mix given that marketing is much more **customer-oriented** than before. These **additional** 3 Ps are particularly **relevant** for the service sector.

People

Anyone who comes into contact with the customer will make an impression that can have a **profound** effect—**positive** or **negative**—on customer satisfaction. Employees and anyone from the company in contact with customers must be **properly** trained. The attitude towards the customer and the level of after-sale support reflect on the company and add value to the product.

Process

This is the element of the marketing mix that considers the systems which are used to **deliver** a service, although it is also linked to the people who provide the service. Clearly defined and efficient processes for things like identifying customer needs or handling orders and customer **complaints** will mean a **consistent**, good quality service. This will then lead to customer loyalty and confidence in the company.

Physical Evidence

This refers to where the service is being delivered from, so it is particularly important for **retailers**, hotels and restaurants for example, although the same concept can be applied to e-stores and websites. A well-designed shop **layout**, with a high level of presentation and excellent standards will mean walking into the shop is a positive experience for customers. A service cannot be experienced before it is delivered, so it is **vital** to ensure customers feel confident in the company and what it offers.

customer-oriented		
	adj.	顾客导向的; 以顾客为中心的
additional	adj.	附加的, 额外的, 外加的
relevant	adj.	紧密相关的; 有价值的; 有意义的
profound	adj.	巨大的; 深远的
positive	adj.	积极的, 正面的
negative	adj.	消极的, 负面的
properly	adv.	正确地; 适当地

deliver	v.	交付; 递送
complaint	n.	投诉; 抱怨
consistent	adj.	始终如一的; 持续的
physical	adj.	实物的; 有形的
evidence	n.	证明; 证据
retailer	n.	零售商; 零售店
layout	n.	布局; 布置; 设计
vital	adj.	必不可少的; 对……极重要的

13 Read the text and answer these questions.

1) What are the three extra Ps and why were they added to the marketing mix?

_____

2) Why is staff training important?

_____

3) What does "process" refer to?

_____

4) How can the systems which are used to deliver a service help customer loyalty?

_____

5) Is "physical evidence" only significant to physical shops and places? Why / Why not?

_____

6) How can "physical evidence" help customers have a positive experience?

_____

14 Translate the following words and expressions into Chinese.

1) value   _____

2) pricing strategy   _____

3) distribution channel   _____

4) buyer behaviour   _____

5) relationship marketing   _____

6) customer satisfaction   _____

7) after-sale support   _____

8) customer loyalty   _____

Speaking 3

15 **What physical evidence would reassure you in these situations? Talk together.**

- It is the first time that you buy something from an online shop that you have never heard of before.

- You want a new look so you walk into a new hair salon.

- You are on holiday and walk into a restaurant for lunch.

Thinking

16 **Read the following text from BBC news. Do you think live-streaming can boost China's economy? Learn and think.**

This business model is not just a top-down effort. Even before officials began appearing on live-streaming services, savvy business owners were turning to live-streaming platforms such as Douyin and Kuaishou, as well as e-commerce giant Alibaba's Taobao, to promote and sell their products in real time.

One of them is 27-year-old Li Jiaqi, whose maverick sales technique has won him the nickname "Lipstick Brother No 1"(口红一哥). Once an unassuming shop assistant earning a modest salary in Nanchang, Jiangxi, he now has more than 40 million followers on Douyin.

In one of his live-streaming sales sessions he sold 15,000 lipsticks within five minutes. Unlike many beauty bloggers he always demonstrates the lipsticks he's selling on his lips, rather than his arms. It seems to be paying off, as he now reportedly has a net worth of up to $5m (£4m).

There is also 33-year-old Wei Ya, whose 1 April sale of a $6m rocket launch on Taobao amazed the nation and attracted international publicity. So much so that Taobao had to issue a statement confirming the sale was real and not an April Fools' joke.

Wei Ya has been a familiar face in China's live-streaming sales circle. Her followers call her "Queen of Goods"(带货女王).

The official *China Daily* says this was "the world's first live broadcast of a rocket sale". More than 620,000 Weibo users have used the tag #WeiYaSellsARocket and more than two million online viewers tuned in to watch the sale.

Foreign brands too have been joining in. Luxury product maker Louis Vuitton hosted a live-streaming sale in March—the first time since the brand entered the Chinese market 30 years ago.

Useful Expressions and Terms

identify customer needs 识别顾客需求

make a profit 获取利润

consumer's requirements 消费者的需求

market research 市场调查

marketing process 营销过程

reduce overall profits 减少总利润

attract / appeal to new customers 吸引新客户

generate optimum profits 产生最大利润

marketing mix 营销组合

generate a revenue 创收

provide a profit 获得利润

cost-plus pricing 成本加利润定价法

profit mark-up 利润加价

potential customer 潜在客户

distribution channel 分销渠道

buyer behaviour 购买者的行为

public relation 公共关系

improve a company's image 改善公司形象

launch a new product 推出新产品

increase popularity of existing products 提高现有产品的知名度

consumer-oriented model 以消费者为导向的模式

relational marketing 关系营销

marketing strategy 营销策略

transactional marketing 交易营销

have a profound effect 产生深刻的影响

customer satisfaction 顾客满意度

the level of after-sale support 售后支持的水平

reflect on the company 反映了公司（的形象）

deliver/provide a service 提供服务

handle orders 处理订单

customer complaint 客户投诉

good quality service 优质服务

customer loyalty 客户忠诚度

well-designed shop layout 精心设计的店铺布局

feel confident in the company 对公司有信心

Learning Objectives

Upon completion of the unit, students will be able to:

- define SWOT analysis and product life cycle;
- use SWOT matrix and identify each stage of the product life cycle to develop a company's strategies;
- write a SWOT analysis for a company or a specific product;
- have professional abilities and good communication skills in problem analysis.

Starting Off

Facing some difficulties in marketing a product, would you choose to analyse internal or external business environment or both? PEST and SWOT are closely related approaches to business analysis. PEST is an acronym that stands for political, economic, social and technological influences on a business. SWOT is a situational analysis tool for company leaders that involves assessing strengths, weaknesses, opportunities and threats. PEST focuses on external environmental factors that affect the business, whereas SWOT analysis focuses on both internal and external factors. PEST explores the political and legal landscape by looking at employment laws, political issues, taxes and regulations that impact the business. What do you think the most important factor is in a marketing campaign? Let's go on and explore more.

Speaking 1

1 **What do you think a company's strengths and weaknesses could be? Talk together.**

Listening

2 **Listen to the following short passage and fill in the blanks.**

A weakness of the SWOT technique is that it can be highly (1)_____. Some factors will always be easy to (2)_____. However, some factors can be either strengths or weaknesses depending upon the business (3)_____. The strength of the SWOT analysis comes from the fact that it can be (4)_____ to many different organisational scenarios, but its weakness is that it requires clear thinking and good (5)_____ to obtain any real (6)_____ from using it. When you are using the SWOT analysis technique, the processes of clearly (7)_____ the business objective and categorising the SWOT factors are (8)_____ important because they are interdependent.

SWOT is an **acronym** that stands for **strengths**, **weaknesses**, **opportunities** and **threats**. It is used in problem analysis and is a common tool used in the business world for marketing analysis. It takes into account both the internal and the external business environment to anticipate possible future actions that may be needed to **defend** or **expand** a company's market position. It takes place during the first stages of planning and helps marketers focus on key issues.

Strengths

They are the company's **resources** and **capabilities** that can be used for developing a **competitive** advantage. Examples of strengths include strong brand names, **patents**, technological skills, cost advantages from **proprietary** know-how, good **reputation**, favourable access to distribution channel and production quality.

Weaknesses (or limitations)

The **absence** of certain strengths (such as those previously mentioned) are considered weaknesses and place the company at a disadvantage.

Opportunities

They are external chances (i.e. from outside the company) to improve **performances** and profits, such as technological improvements, change in demographics, the **liberalisation** of **regulations** and the **elimination** of international trade barriers.

Threats

External elements that could cause trouble to the business may include consumer tastes moving away from the company's products, the emergence of **substitute** products, new regulations, increased trade barriers, natural disasters and **downturn** in the global economy.

The SWOT (or TOWS) **matrix** shown in the table below is used to develop the company's strategies in order to improve its situation.

Companies may use:

S-O strategies: They pursue opportunities which match the company's strengths;

W-O strategies: They **overcome** weaknesses to pursue opportunities;

S-T strategies: They identify plans enabling the company to use its strengths to reduce its **exposure** to external threats;

W-T strategies: They establish a

	Strengths	Weaknesses
Opportunities	S-O strategies	W-O strategies
Threats	S-T strategies	W-T strategies

defensive plan to prevent the company's weaknesses from making it highly **vulnerable** to threats.

acronym	n.	首字母缩略词	reputation	n.	名誉, 名声
strength	n.	优点, 优势	absence	n.	缺乏, 没有
weakness	n.	弱点, 劣势	performance	n.	业绩; 工作情况
opportunity	n.	机会, 时机	liberalisation	n.	自由化; 开放
threat	n.	挑战; 恐吓	regulation	n.	章程; 规章制度
defend	v.	保住, 保护	elimination	n.	消除; 淘汰; 除去
expand	v.	扩大; 提升; 增强	substitute	n.	代替者; 代替物
resource	n.	资源; 财力	downturn	n.	（商业经济的）衰退; 衰退期
capability	n.	能力, 才能	matrix	n.	矩阵; 模型
competitive	adj.	竞争的; 竞争性的	overcome	v.	克服; 解决
patent	n.	专利权; 专利证书	exposure	n.	面临; 遭受
proprietary	adj.	专卖的, 专营的	vulnerable	adj.	脆弱的; 易受伤害的

3 Read the text and answer these questions.

1) Why is SWOT analysis used in marketing?

_____

2) At what stage is it used?

_____

3) Which are internal factors and which are external factors?

_____

4) Give two examples of strengths/weaknesses.

_____

5) Give two examples of opportunities/threats.

_____

4 Fill in the blanks with words or expressions from the box, changing the form if necessary.

downturn	good reputation	production quality	trade barriers
marketer	market position	substitute products	brand

1) He is a salesman, a _____ and a merchant, and he always thought he could tell Starbucks' story best.

2) Solid internal and external growth allows us to expand our _____ in both developing and mature markets.

3) The company relocated its market position to change its _____ image.

4) _____ from smaller, more agile companies have a history of upending the established players.

5) Brands with a _____, such as Mercedes-Benz, can survive a hiccup or two without too much damage.

6) The _____ of the film was really ordinary, which surprised me.

7) Today, because of advances in technology and falling _____, information and ideas circle the globe faster and more freely than ever.

8) The unprecedented _____ in key resource prices is potentially dislocating markets across the globe.

5 Translate the following expressions into Chinese.

1) proprietary know-how   _____

2) distribution channel   _____

3) downturn in the global economy   _____

4) strong brand name   _____

5) cost advantages   _____

6) technological improvements   _____

7) change in demographics   _____

8) liberalisation of regulations   _____

9) the elimination of international trade barriers   _____

10) new regulations   _____

6 Decide if the following are strengths (*S*), weaknesses (*W*), opportunities (*O*) or threats (*T*).

1) The company's production facilities are located far from its customer base. ☐

2) The company has grown substantially over recent years, and has experienced global expansion. ☐

3) A company producing software is dependent upon another company's research. ☐

4) There are new and emerging markets. ☐

5) To expand its brand, the company sells its name to makers of apparel, watches, sunglasses, etc. ☐

6) The company's products are vulnerable to the uncertainty of the job market because of the weakened economy. ☐

7) A large company has significant cost advantages over most of their competitors. ☐

8) There are religious, cultural and social restrictions in the new markets. ☐

Reading 2

Within the context of tourism and **hospitality**, a SWOT analysis can be used by a national tourism organisation deciding how to promote the country or a particular area, and also by companies, such as tour **operators** and hotel **chains**, which are considering adding new products or promoting new **destinations**. Below is an example of different factors that could be included in a SWOT analysis for a tourist destination.

	POSITIVE	**NEGATIVE**
INTERNAL	**STRENGTHS** **Resources and capabilities that can be used to develop a competitive advantage** • cultural and historical heritage • beauty of unique natural environment • well-established local traditions • knowledge of English by local people	**WEAKNESSES** **Limitations or situations that place the area at a disadvantage** • lack of trained local staff • high levels of pollution • risks to the safety and security of tourists • **scarce** water supply
EXTERNAL	**OPPORTUNITIES** **External chances to improve and increase** • plans for a new airport • improved **infrastructure** in the area • liberalisation of an industry/market • growth in a particular form of tourism, e.g. medical	**THREATS** **External factors that could cause trouble or problems** • changes to local **legislation** • political **instability** • natural disasters • competition from a **neighbouring** destination

S W O T

MY GLOSSARY

hospitality	*n.*	服务; 款待
operator	*n.*	经营者; 专业公司
chain	*n.*	连锁商店
destination	*n.*	目的地; 终点
scarce	*adj.*	缺乏的, 不足的

infrastructure	*n.*	基础设施; 基础建设
legislation	*n.*	法规; 法律
instability	*n.*	不稳定; 不稳固
neighbouring	*adj.*	邻近的, 附近的, 毗邻的

7 In pairs, complete this SWOT analysis for a tour operator that is considering launching a new package tour in the Caribbean.

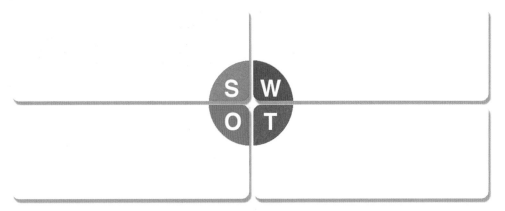

1) tour operator has 15 years' experience in the Caribbean

2) low profits for the last two years

3) changes to local tax laws

4) cultural differences

5) very strong competition on the island

6) hurricanes and tropical storms

7) limited infrastructure on the island

8) brand name well associated with quality

Writing

8 Choose a specific product you like, a brand, a company or even your own school, and complete a brief SWOT chart.

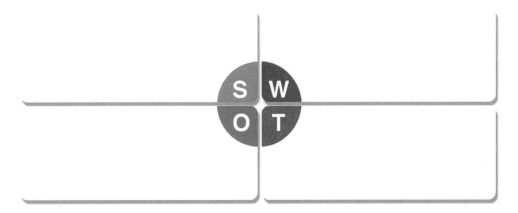

9 Give a brief SWOT analysis according to the information below.

a You have 3 years' experience of a commodity promoter, selling products on Taobao's online live-broadcasting platform.

b You have learned a course on photography techniques.

c Your store is away from the crowded downtown area.

d You start a live-streaming session where you introduce the clothes in your store.

e The Internet has made the market flat, and live-streaming can help your products reach more potential customers.

f The decentralised Internet has blurred the difference between opening a store downtown and in suburban areas.

g Live-streaming has become a trend not only for Chinese online shopping platforms such as Taobao but also for entity stores.

h More than 100,000 online shops provided a live broadcast for consumer interaction.

i It's more time-saving to shop through the live-streaming alternative.

j You can interact with the viewer instead of only browsing the introduction pages.

Strengths: _____

Weaknesses: _____

Opportunities: _____

Threats: _____

10 You want to carry out promotional activities during this year's Singles' Day shopping spree. Write your marketing strategies according to your analyses.

S-O strategies: _____

W-O strategies: _____

S-T strategies: _____

W-T strategies: _____

11 What do you think the life cycle of a product is? Do you think it is the same for all products? Discuss with your partner.

Reading 3

Product Life Cycle

Products pass through different phases during their life **cycle** and each stage normally requires adjustments to the marketing mix in order to face the challenges and opportunities which **arise**.

Introduction on the Market

After a period of development, probably with **substantial** research and development costs, the product is launched on the market. At this **phase** the product is **promoted** to create awareness. Limited numbers of products are available in few channels of distribution. Costs are very high, while sales **volumes** are low. Careful **monitoring** of a product's growth at this stage is **essential**.

Growth

During this stage, public awareness as well as sales volumes rapidly increase and the product becomes more profitable. Distribution becomes more widespread. As competitors are attracted into the market with very similar offerings, competition begins to increase. Promotion and advertising costs are high and focus upon building the brand.

Maturity

At this stage, sales volumes **peak** and the market reaches **saturation**. Competition is the most **intense** and companies fight to defend their market **share** and maximise profit. Producers attempt to **differentiate** products, adding new features or services or improving quality. Prices normally drop due to the increased competition. Promotion is widespread and carefully monitored against what competitors are doing. Some producers may begin to leave the market due to poor profit **margins**.

Decline

At this point there is a downturn in the market. The introduction of more **innovative** products or the change in consumer tastes cause sales volumes to decline. There are various possibilities available to a company: **rejuvenate** the product, **dramatically** cut costs (e.g. by finding a cheaper production **facility**), sell the product in an alternative market. Ultimately if a product is unprofitable, a company will **withdraw** it from the market.

Not all products, however, go through all phases and the length of each phase also varies enormously. Some fad products can go straight from introduction to quick decline. Others, such as the car, have an extremely long mature stage. In addition, the decisions of market strategists can influence the different phases, both positively and negatively.

MY GLOSSARY

cycle	n.	周期; 循环
arise	v.	产生, 出现; 发生
introduction	n.	初次投入使用; 采用; 引进
substantial	adj.	大量的; 很大程度的
phase	n.	阶段; 时期
promote	v.	促销; 推销
volume	n.	量; 额
monitor	v.	监控; 监视; 跟踪调查
essential	adj.	完全必要的; 必不可少的
maturity	n.	成熟; 成熟期
peak	v.	达到高峰; 达到最高值

saturation	n.	饱和; 饱和状态
intense	adj.	剧烈的; 十分强烈的
share	n.	份额; 股份
differentiate	v.	区分, 区别, 辨别
margin	n.	利润幅度; 毛利
innovative	adj.	革新的, 创新的; 采用新方法的
rejuvenate	v.	使更新; 使年轻; 使更有活力
dramatically	adv.	显著地; 剧烈地
facility	n.	设施; 设备; (服务等的)特色
withdraw	v.	撤回, 撤离

12 Complete the following sentences with the words from this unit. Some letters have been given.

1) The life cycle of a product is divided into four stages—in_____, growth, maturity and decline.

2) The life c_____ of a product is used by marketing professionals as a factor in deciding when it is appropriate to increase advertising, reduce prices, expand to new markets, or redesign packaging.

3) And 100 percent of consumers dif_____ between brands of facial soap.

4) The concept of product life cycle helps inform business decision-making, from pricing and pro_____ to expansion or cost-cutting.

5) This introduction phase generally includes a sub_____ investment in advertising and a marketing campaign focused on making consumers aware of the product and its benefits.

6) The g_____ stage is characterised by growing demand, an increase in production, and expansion in its availability.

7) The most profitable stage is ma_____, while the costs of producing and marketing decline.

8) The product may lose market sh_____ and begin its decline at the fourth stage.

13 Which phase(s) of the product life cycle do these steps belong to?

	Introduction	Growth	Maturity	Decline
1) Public awareness increases	☐	☐	☐	☐
2) Sales volumes peak	☐	☐	☐	☐
3) Withdrawal from the market	☐	☐	☐	☐
4) Costs are very high	☐	☐	☐	☐
5) Market share becomes stable	☐	☐	☐	☐
6) Promotion	☐	☐	☐	☐

Thinking

14 **The following is about the importance of product life cycle. Could you find more examples about extending the product life cycle? Learn and think.**

We can see how the product life cycle works by looking at the introduction of instant (速溶) coffee. When it was introduced, most people did not like it and it took several years to gain general acceptance (introduction stage). At one point, though, instant coffee grew rapidly in popularity, and many brands were introduced (stage of rapid growth). After a while, people became attached to one brand and sales levelled off (stage of maturity). Sales went into a slight decrease when freeze-dried coffees were introduced (stage of decline).

The importance of the product life cycle to marketers is this: Different stages in the product life cycle call for different strategies. The goal is to extend the product life so that sales and profits do not drop. One strategy is called market modification. It means that marketing managers look for new users and market sections. It also means searching for increased usage among present customers or going for a different market, such as senior citizens. A marketer may reposition the product to appeal to new market sections.

Another product extension strategy is called product modification. It involves changing product quality, features, or style to attract new users or more usage from present users.

Useful Expressions and Terms

SWOT analysis SWOT 分析

marketing analysis 营销分析

take into account 考虑

expand a company's market position 提升公司的
市场地位

focus on key issues 关注主要问题

competitive advantage 竞争优势

strong brand names 大品牌

technological skill 技术技能

cost advantage 成本优势

proprietary know-how 专有技术

good reputation 好名声

production quality 生产质量

technological improvement 技术改进

the liberalisation of regulations 放宽管制

the elimination of international trade barriers 消除
国际贸易壁垒

natural disaster 自然灾害

downturn in the global economy 全球经济低迷

tour operator 旅游运营商

hotel chain 连锁酒店

tourist destination 旅游目的地

high level of pollution 高度污染

lack of trained local staff 缺乏训练有素的当地员工

political instability 政治的不稳定性

online live-broadcasting platform 在线直播平台

the crowded downtown area 拥挤的市中心

start a live-streaming session 发起一个直播会话

suburban area 郊区

entity store 实体店

consumer interaction 消费者互动

the life cycle of a product 产品的生命周期

create awareness 创造知名度

sales volume 销量

careful monitoring of a product's growth 严密监控
产品增长期

public awareness 公众认知度

similar offering 相似的产品

build the brand 品牌建设

maximise profit 利润最大化

differentiate products 区分产品

add new features or services 添加新功能或服务

improve quality 提高质量

poor profit margins 利润低

rejuvenate the product 更新产品

dramatically cut costs 大幅削减费用

production facility 生产设备

Market Research and Analysing Data

Learning Objectives

Upon completion of the unit, students will be able to:

- define market research and know the advantages and disadvantages of two types of data sources, digital marketing and the primary research methods;

- conduct a primary market research to develop an effective marketing strategy;

- describe data changes and trends in charts and graphs and fill in a marketing questionnaire based on the situation;

- have professional abilities and good communication skills in market research and analysing data.

Starting Off

What is market research? Who conducts market research? Market research is the process of determining the viability of a new product or service. It can be done through surveys, product testing and focus groups by the company itself, or by a third-party company that specialises in market research. The following is a common process of working: conduct desk research to gather background market information; develop research methodology and objectives; recruit respondents; gather data and information from respondents; analyse research information; prepare research reports. Let's go on and explore more.

Reading 1

Market research is the collection of data from various sources in order to obtain information regarding the needs and wants of customers and the structure and **dynamics** of a particular market. It is an essential part of defining a market strategy.

There are two types of data sources:

Primary Data (also known as field research)

This is research that is **conceived** for a specific objective and is collected first hand through **observation**, experiment or **surveys**, such as face-to-face interviews and online **questionnaires**. This form of research provides specific data which is extremely relevant to the company. The sample size interviewed must be large enough to provide data that **accurately** reflects the market. For this reason, field research is an expensive and time-consuming option.

Secondary Data (also known as desk research)

Secondary data is existing information so it is a cheaper and quicker source than field research. However, it is important to check how up-to-date, accurate, **reliable** and relevant to the specific needs the information actually is. Secondary data can be internal to the company, such as sales records and customer reports, or external. Examples of secondary data include statistics from trade organisations or government reports, articles and market reports. The Internet is also an important source of secondary data with sites silently tracking user behaviour and preferences, as well as selling market research reports.

Organisations may decide to conduct market research either themselves or through an independent marketing research firm. Whatever the means, before **undertaking** any research project it is crucial to define the research objectives and then to analyse and **interpret** the data correctly in order to develop an effective marketing strategy.

Quantitative research uses statistics and **numerical** data. Qualitative research is more **subjective** and concentrates on the hows and whys of things.

MY GLOSSARY

dynamics	n.	动态; 动力
conceive	v.	构想, 设想
observation	n.	观察, 观测
survey	n.	调查; 测量
questionnaire	n.	调查表; 问卷
accurately	adv.	精确地, 准确地

reliable	adj.	真实可信的; 可靠的
undertake	v.	承担; 从事; 负责
interpret	v.	诠释; 说明
numerical	adj.	数字的; 用数字表示的
subjective	adj.	主观的; 个人的

1 Read the text and complete the table below.

	Primary Data	Secondary Data
Examples	*face-to-face interview*	
Advantages		
Disadvantages		

2 **Look at this bar chart and answer these questions.**

Inbound visitors to the UK who undertake an English language course

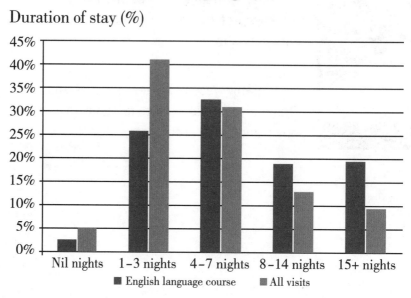

Duration of stay (%)

Legend: ■ English language course ■ All visits

1) What does the graph represent?

_____

2) What is the most common length of trip for those doing an English language course and for all visitors?

_____

3) How does the percentage of visitors who stay for more than two weeks compare between the two categories?

_____

Reading **2**

Digital Marketing

Digital marketing—the promotion of products, brands and services using electronic media—has dramatically changed the face of marketing. It is relatively cheap, compared to traditional media, and so is the ideal tool for any business, be it the largest **multinational** or a **start-up** fashion designer selling T-shirts from a **basement**. It provides vast quantities of data on things like a user's shopping habits, interests and physical movements through the use of cookies, tracking codes and data collection on apps so that a company can target a specific audience.

Digital marketers can monitor and analyse this data—practically in real time—and can adjust marketing campaigns **accordingly**.

Digital marketing techniques include Internet-based activities like search engine **optimisation** and digital display advertising on websites, games **consoles** with in-game advertising, digital television, social media marketing and mobile phone marketing. Social media marketing allows a company to follow things like Twitter and Facebook comments to find out what people think about a product or a service, and also to develop a fan base

of followers. This means they can then accurately aim advertising at an extremely specific target. This can be through mobile web access, but also SMS, MMS, push **notifications**, QR codes, mobile apps and location-based marketing.

However, there are also some **obstacles** that might limit the success of digital marketing. There is so much competition from businesses of all kinds and sizes that it is becoming much more difficult to **capture** the attention of the user. Lastly, it can be extremely **problematic** for a company to use correctly and effectively the **sheer** amount of data available from all these digital sources.

MY GLOSSARY

multinational	adj.	跨国的; 多国的
start-up	adj.	启动时期的; 开始阶段的
basement	n.	地下室; 地窖
accordingly	adv.	相应地; 照着
optimisation	n.	最佳化, 最优化
console	n.	控制台; 仪表板

notification	n.	通知; 通告
obstacle	n.	阻碍; 绊脚石
capture	v.	引起(注意、想象、兴趣等)
problematic	adj.	造成困难的; 产生问题的
sheer	adj.	绝对的; 纯粹的

3 Read the text and decide if these sentences are true (*T*) or false (*F*). If there is not enough information, choose "doesn't say" (*DS*).

	T	F	DS
1) Digital marketing costs much more than traditional marketing.	☐	☐	☐
2) It is only useful for large multinationals.	☐	☐	☐
3) Collecting data through digital channels is considered to be an invasion of privacy.	☐	☐	☐
4) Social media and mobile marketing are expected to expand.	☐	☐	☐
5) Companies use social media to know people's opinions and ideas.	☐	☐	☐
6) It is not possible to target a precise audience with mobile marketing.	☐	☐	☐
7) Increased competition can reduce the success of digital marketing.	☐	☐	☐
8) Consumers want to use devices that limit the amount of digital marketing they receive.	☐	☐	☐

4 Find the verbs in the text for these definitions.

1) to select as an object of attention   _____

2) to watch something carefully and record the results   _____

3) to look and think about something in order to understand it   _____

4) to change something slightly   _____

5) to learn or discover a fact   _____

6) to restrict or get in the way   _____

Reading 3

Primary Research Methods

Questionnaires

A questionnaire is an **inexpensive** and fast method for gathering a large amount of data in a short period of time. The questions must be designed so that they are easy to understand and provide a clear and **unambiguous** outcome. Nowadays most questionnaires are online and are often to check customer satisfaction with a purchased product or to obtain suggestions, **feedback** and opinions. One disadvantage with questionnaires sent by post or email is that it is a passive method relying on people to complete and send back the form.

Street Interviews

Common places for street interviews are busy streets in town centres and shopping malls. A researcher will stop a person and ask a few **preliminary** questions, known as **screening** questions, to ensure that the sample of people interviewed is **representative**. The interaction may end after this or continue with the full interview. Although an effective method of data collection, it is not always the most cost effective as it involves paying the researchers for their time and not every interaction turns out to be a useful interview.

Phone Interviews

When conducting phone interviews, the interviewee may be selected randomly from a database or chosen as part of a specific target market or demographic group. The interviewer's questions need to be ordered correctly so as not to **prejudice** the interviewee's views. For example, asking "Do you like XYZ Tea?" before you ask "Which teas are you aware of?" will prejudice the answers. A major disadvantage of this kind of research method is that many people are **reluctant** to waste their time answering questions and may be **wary** of the real purpose of the phone call.

Focus Group

This is the most common form of research when a company needs to know all about consumers' opinions and it is widely used for both services and products. The discussion among a group of about 6–12 people has to be led by a trained **moderator** who can guide the conversation from a general discussion to one that focuses on the specific topic. All members of the group must feel comfortable and be given a chance to speak as the interaction and exchange of ideas, opinions and attitudes are fundamental.

Consumer Panel

A consumer panel is made up of a selected group of consumers from a specific market **sector** who give their opinions on a particular product or service. Consumer panels are often used to test a product before a **launch**. The same people are often used on a continuous basis and they can give their feedback in person or in the form of written **comments**.

Product Test

This form of research is particularly used in the consumer markets. The manufacturer selects a group of potential buyers and offers a sample for people to use, on agreement that they report back their findings. This could be done over a period of time while using the product at home or just on one day, for example food tasting outside a supermarket.

MY GLOSSARY

inexpensive	*adj.*	廉价的, 不贵的
unambiguous	*adj.*	意思清楚的; 明确的
feedback	*n.*	反馈的意见（或信息）
preliminary	*adj.*	预备的; 初步的
screening	*n.*	筛查

representative	adj.	典型的; 有代表性的	moderator	n.	调解人, 调停人
prejudice	n.	偏见, 成见	sector	n.	领域; 行业; 部门
reluctant	adj.	不情愿的, 勉强的	launch	n.	产品发布; 投放市场
wary	adj.	小心的, 谨慎的	comment	n.	评论; 解释

5 Read the text and answer these questions.

1) What are the advantages and disadvantages of questionnaires?

_____

2) What are screening questions and why are they used in interviews?

_____

3) What are the disadvantages of street interviews?

_____

4) In what way can the order of questions in interviews prejudice the answers?

_____

5) What is the difference between a focus group and a consumer panel?

_____

6) How are product tests carried out?

_____

6 Fill in the blanks with words or expressions from the box, changing the form if necessary.

research	phone interview	survey	questionnaire	digital marketing
online	product test	panel	focus group	primary

1) _____ information is the data that the company has collected directly or that has been collected by a person or business hired to conduct the research.

2) Secondary information is data that an outside entity has already gathered, which can include population information from government census data and trade association _____ reports.

3) With so many great opportunities for using _____, it can be difficult to know which to prioritise.

4) Data collected from these interviews were compared with the amount of distribution of the publication in order to see how effective those ads were. Market research and _____ were adapted from these early techniques.

5) _____ could collect information or organise focus groups—and do so quickly and in a more organised and orderly fashion.

6) Many market research activities have shifted _____ as well with people spending more time online, instead of companies actively seeking participants by finding them on the street or by cold calling them on the phone.

7) By taking a step-by-step approach to _____ development, you can come up with an effective means to collect data that will answer your unique research question.

8) To complement purchase and usage behavioural information with new viewpoints on consumers' opinions and attitudes, we can speak with our _____ members.

9) This paper examines some of the methodological issues raised by the collection and analysis of _____ data.

10) Product technical data are only for customers' reference, which cannot be used as an indicator basis for _____.

7 **Look at this extract from a focus group discussing different kinds of restaurants. Complete the conversation using the expressions in the box. More than one answer is possible.**

What's your opinion	What about...	What do you think...	I think...
In my opinion	according to...	You're right	I think so too
I absolutely agree	I agree up to a point	I see what you mean	I totally disagree

Moderator: (1) _____ about the atmosphere in these kinds of restaurants?

Rachel: (2) _____, the atmosphere in a steak house is great. I like that vibe.

Robert: (3) _____, but I feel that sometimes they're not really very authentic.

Moderator: (4) _____ the food?

Robert: (5) _____ the choice is wider in a steak house, but (6) _____ an article I read they use a lot of frozen food. A pizzeria offers much fresher food.

Anne: (7) _____. It's healthier too.

Rachel: (8) _____. That's the biggest problem with fast food places. Everything's fried.

Robert: (9) _____, but they are cheap.

Anne: Yes. (10) _____! And price is important.

Moderator: (11) _____?

Tom: (12) _____. Price isn't important at all. Quality should be the first thing to look at.

Listening

8 Listen to five extracts from a focus group discussing mobile phone service providers. Match each speaker to what he/she is talking about. There are three options that you do not need.

a   poor Internet access

b   the quality of customer service

c   the transparency of contracts

d   the choice of mobile phone models

e   the importance of staying up-to-date

f   the possibility to make phone calls anywhere

g   better deals for existing customers

h   improved services for businesses

Speaker 1 ☐

Speaker 2 ☐

Speaker 3 ☐

Speaker 4 ☐

Speaker 5 ☐

Speaking 1

9 Work in small groups. You are part of a focus group talking about tablets. Choose one of the group to be the moderator. Now share your opinions, ideas and thoughts about tablets. Use these points to help you.

> how easy it is to use   optional features
>
> price   fundamental features
>
> quality   design   size
>
> things you like/dislike

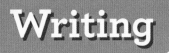
Writing

10 Look at the questionnaire and discuss the questions below.

Thank you for purchasing our products. Please take a few moments to complete a brief survey to help us in our effort to improve our website. Thank you!

1 How did you find out about our website?

☐ Friends' recommendation   ☐ Link in email   ☐ Link from a different website   ☐ TV ad
☐ Radio ad   ☐ Newspaper/Magazine ad   ☐ Online ad   ☐ Search engine ad
☐ Search engine result   ☐ Social networking ad   ☐ Other, please specify: _____

2 How would you rate your experience with our website?

☐ excellent   ☐ very good   ☐ neutral   ☐ poor   ☐ very poor

3 How would you rate our website compared with other websites selling similar products?

	excellent	very good	neutral	poor	very poor
Website design/look	☐	☐	☐	☐	☐
Website navigation	☐	☐	☐	☐	☐
Product selection	☐	☐	☐	☐	☐
Product description/information	☐	☐	☐	☐	☐
Product images	☐	☐	☐	☐	☐
Product pricing	☐	☐	☐	☐	☐
Product ordering	☐	☐	☐	☐	☐
Shipping options	☐	☐	☐	☐	☐
Shipping price	☐	☐	☐	☐	☐
Return policy/information	☐	☐	☐	☐	☐
Contact information	☐	☐	☐	☐	☐
Customer service	☐	☐	☐	☐	☐

4 Would you recommend our website to others?

☐ yes   ☐ maybe   ☐ no

5 Do you expect to use our website again in the future?

☐ definitely   ☐ possibly   ☐ unlikely   ☐ no

---

1) Why are the questions with options to tick rather than open questions?

2) Who is the questionnaire aimed at?

3) What is the purpose of the questionnaire?

4) How might the company use the information from Question 1?

11 Fill in the questionnaire above based on this situation.

A friend of yours suggested you buy a sweatshirt from a website that offers a wide range of goods. The site was easy to navigate with a cool design, and offered a wide selection of shipping options at good prices. You bought the sweatshirt at a really good price but you were not at all satisfied with your purchase. The product description was misleading and the order took seven working days longer than promised.

Reading 4

Most of the data used in market research is presented in different types of **tables** and **charts** in order to make it easier to understand and quicker to compare results, trends and **forecasts**. The most common forms for presenting data and statistics are:

Bar Chart This uses **horizontal** or **vertical** bars to compare things between different groups and also to follow changes over time.

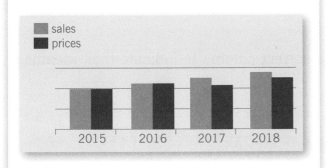

Line Graph This type of graph shows trends or changes over a period of time, particularly when the changes are small, with a horizontal **axis** (x) which shows time and a vertical axis (y) which shows different data, for example the number of visitors, sales or income.

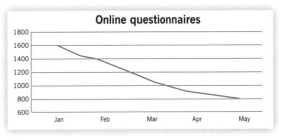

Table This shows numerical data in **columns** and rows.

Product Test	
Feature	**Percentage**
Ease of use	18
Large screen	25
Choice of colours	47
Waterproof	48
Memory capacity	38
Voice recognition	29
Cross device compatibility	33

Pie Chart This is a circle, divided into **segments**, which shows parts of a whole and does not show changes over time.

Visits to the UK (2016)

Purpose	Visits	% of total
Holiday	13.89 m	36.94%
Business	9.19 m	24.43%
VFR	11.57 m	30.77%
Study	526,284	1.41%
Miscellaneous	2.43 m	6.45%
Total	37.61 m	100%

MY GLOSSARY

table	*n.* 表格	vertical	*adj.* 垂直的; 竖的
chart	*n.* 图表	axis	*n.* 轴
forecast	*n.* 预测; 预报	column	*n.* 列; 纵队
horizontal	*adj.* 水平的; 地平线的	segment	*n.* 部分; 段

12 Match each of these sentences to the most suitable chart.

1) Analysing 2016, we can see that the biggest motivation for travel to the UK was for a holiday with nearly 37%, followed by visiting friends and family with nearly 31%.

_____

2) Over the four year period in question, sales increased steadily. Prices showed a similar trend, although they decreased slightly in 2017.

_____

3) From an analysis of the product test, it is clear that users primarily appreciated the choice of colours and the waterproof nature of the device.

_____

4) In the first five months of the year, the number of online questionnaires that were completed continued to fall.

_____

13 Put these words and expressions into the correct column to indicate their meaning.

go up	increase	go down	decrease	fall	decline	grow
stabilise	drop	rise	improve	level off	peak	plummet
steady	jump	pick up	climb	remain constant	become stable	soar
recover	rally	boom	dip	rocket	plunge	crash

↑	→	↓
rise, _____	level off, _____	plummet, _____

14 Look at the sentences in the first column and complete their opposites by choosing the words and expressions from the box.

> has changed   rose   decrease   lowest ever rate   fell dramatically   have been lowered

1) Sales grew rapidly in the first quarter.   ⟷ Sales _____ in the first three months of the year.

2) Advertising costs reached a peak in July.   ⟷ July saw advertising costs at their _____.

3) Our market share has remained constant.   ⟷ Our share of the market _____.

4) There has been a 1% rise in interest rates. ⟷ Interest rates _____ by 1%.

5) Customer complaints have increased sharply this month.   ⟷ There has been a significant _____ in customer complaints this month.

6) The price of mobile phones dropped by 9%. ⟷ Mobile phone prices _____ by 9%.

Speaking 2

15 Why do you think data, such as financial reports, market research statistics and sales records, is presented in tables and charts and graphs?

16 Take turns to describe this graph using the above examples and vocabulary to help you. Talk together.

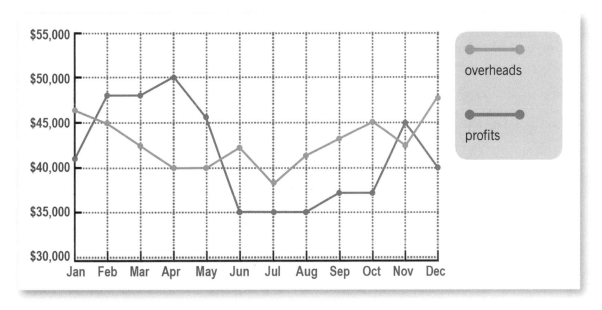

Unit 3   Market Research and Analysing Data   45

Thinking

17 The following is part of a questionnaire for customer satisfaction at McDonald's in Asia. What do you think the most important thing is in a market survey? Learn and think.

Market surveys are an important part of market research that measure the feelings and preferences of customers in a given market. Varying greatly in size, design and purpose, market surveys are one of the main pieces of data that companies and organisations use in determining what products and services to offer and how to market them.

Dear friends,

We are conducting a survey on our master project paper and we need your cooperation to answer this questionnaire. This survey is required to complete our master program. Your information will be regarded strictly confidential and used only for statistical analysis and academic purpose. Your help is very important to this survey and we deeply appreciate your cooperation.

Thank you very much for your help in advance.

1 **What is your gender?**
　☐ male　　　　　　　☐ female

2 **What is your age?**
　☐ below 20　　　☐ 21–30 years old　　　☐ 31–40 years old　　　☐ above 40

3 **What is your education background?**
　☐ high school or below　☐ diploma/certificate/HND　☐ bachelor's degree　☐ master or above

4 **How much is your consumption each month?**
　☐ below ¥1,500　　☐ ¥1,500–¥3,000　　☐ ¥3,500–¥4,500　　☐ above ¥4,500

5 **Which province do you come from in China?**

_____

6 **This following is about exploratory key factors that influence customer satisfaction. Please indicate to which extent you think it is agreeable or disagreeable.**

	Strongly Disagree	Disagree	Neutral	Agree	Strongly Agree
Service quality					
Price					
Taste					
Environment					
Convenience					

Useful Expressions and Terms

dynamics of a particular market 特定市场的动态

define a market strategy 确定市场战略

data source 数据来源

primary data 原始数据

field research 实地调查研究

first hand 第一手地; 直接地

the sample size interviewed 采访的样本量

secondary data 二手资料

desk research 案头研究

user behaviour and preferences 用户行为和偏好

conduct market research 进行市场调查

undertake any research project 承担任何研究项目

quantitative research 定量研究

numerical data 数字数据

qualitative research 定性研究

digital marketing 数字营销

electronic media 电子媒体

tracking code 跟踪代码

data collection on apps 应用程序上的数据收集

search engine optimisation 搜索引擎优化

digital display advertising 数码展示广告

in-game advertising 游戏内置广告

develop a fan base of followers 建立粉丝团

mobile web access 移动网络访问

push notification 推送通知

QR code 二维码

location-based marketing 基于位置的营销

street interview 街头采访

screening question 筛选出的问题

focus group 焦点小组; 小组座谈会

consumer panel 消费者特定小组

product test 产品测试

bar chart 长条图

line graph 线状图表

pie chart 饼状图

vertical axis 纵轴

horizontal axis 横轴

Mail

Learning Objectives

Upon completion of the unit, students will be able to:

- explain different types of unsolicited offers;
- introduce goods or services by using unsolicited offers and know useful language in unsolicited letters, emails and phone calls;
- write an unsolicited letter or email;
- have professional abilities and good communication skills in unsolicited offers.

Starting Off

If you are an email sender, how many emails do you send on a daily basis? Are they effective emails? Right from the get-go, remember the two important pieces of information: short and concise, and then you will make it. First, begin your email with a friendly and engaging greeting, and swiftly move to your promotional offer in the first sentence. Consider adding a call to action to spur further sales such as "In addition, the first 50 people to redeem this offer will receive...". Second, write a compelling subject line for your email that both summarises the content and moves people to open your email promptly. Third, set a reasonable deadline so that readers respond to your offer in a prompt manner. Let's go on and explore more.

Speaking 1

1 **Have you ever received telephone calls, emails or letters promoting a product or a service? Do you just ignore them or do you take note? Talk together.**

Reading 1

A common form of marketing is the use of **unsolicited** letters, **brochures**, **hand-outs** or telephone calls and unsolicited electronic messages in your email **inbox**, on your mobile phone, on social networks, blogs and **forums**. They are distributed broadly and can require no marketing research other than (email) addresses or phone numbers. Mailing lists for these purposes can be purchased from **specialised** companies. The aim of these unsolicited **offers** is to introduce goods or services and they are often **accompanied** by promotional offers in the form of discounts. They are almost always created to **motivate** the **recipient** to do something. It could be to fill out a form, visit a store, make a purchase, visit a website, or to place a telephone call.

While many of us may consider these techniques **irritating**—**interrupting** us as we are about to sit down to dinner or filling up our inboxes with **spam**—enough people obviously take up the various offers to make it a worthwhile and cost-effective marketing method for companies.

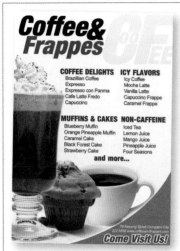

Hand-out or Flier

These are single, small sheets of paper (usually A4 or smaller), handed out **anonymously** at events or on the street. They can also distributed by hand to letterboxes in a neighbourhood. They are brightly-coloured with information regarding a product or service, often with a special offer or discount.

Unsolicited Letter/email

Normally written with strong persuasive language to encourage a particular action by the recipient, they can be sent to specific named individuals or in mass to unknown recipients. They are often called **junk mail** or spam.

Telemarketing

This refers to phone calls made by company staff, or from a call centre, to businesses or private individuals in an attempt to promote and sell products or services. This technique can also be used by market research companies to collect data, political parties to seek support and **charity** organisations for **donations**. The recipients are often **randomly** selected from a database or phone **directory**. **Alternatively**, they can be carefully selected from market studies or data gathered on the Internet on the basis of their demographic, geographic, **psychographic** and behavioural characteristics.

MY GLOSSARY

unsolicited	*adj.*	未经请求的; 主动提供的
brochure	*n.*	手册; 小册子
hand-out	*n.*	宣传册子, 宣传品; 讲义
inbox	*n.*	（电子邮件）收件箱; 收件夹
forum	*n.*	论坛; 讨论会
specialised	*adj.*	专门的; 特别的
offer	*n.*	（通常为短期的）减价, 特价
accompany	*v.*	陪同, 陪伴
motivate	*v.*	激励; 激发

recipient	n.	受方; 接受者	telemarketing	n.	电话营销, 电话销售
irritating	adj.	使愤怒的; 烦人的	charity	n.	慈善机构（或组织）
interrupt	v.	打断; 妨碍	donation	n.	捐赠物; 捐赠; 赠送
spam	n.	滥发的邮件; 垃圾邮件	randomly	adv.	随便地, 任意地
flier	n.	广告传单;飞行物	directory	n.	姓名地址录; 目录
anonymously	adv.	匿名地; 化名地	alternatively	adv.	非此即彼; 或者
junk mail		垃圾邮件; 邮寄宣传品	psychographic	adj.	心理记录的; 人格特征图的

2 Read the text and answer these questions.

1) Why are these types of marketing called unsolicited offers?

_____

2) Where do companies get the details of potential customers?

_____

3) What is the purpose of an unsolicited offer?

_____

4) What reaction do a lot of people have to unsolicited offers?

_____

5) What advantages does this kind of technique have for companies?

_____

6) Can you think of any disadvantages?

_____

3 Fill in the blanks with words from the box, changing the form if necessary.

unsolicited	specialise	spam	directory
interrupt	telemarketing	offer	motivate

1) The _____ ads appear prominently on the screen and are something irritating for many users.

2) Consumers are increasingly looking to save on free shipping and retailers are responding with promotional _____.

3) He had to learn management skills, figuring out how to hire, train and _____ employees for his stores.

4) If you have _____ requirements, consider whether a given product has customisations

suited to that need.

5) We _____ this programme to bring you an important news bulletin.

6) Ten years of retail experience offers much more chance of success than an opportunity based on _____ skills, where you have zero experience.

7) There are many different tools and systems available for the filtering and removal of _____ email at the UNIX server level.

8) The piece of paper you have here is 250 names chosen randomly from a Manhattan phone _____.

Reading 2

CITYBIKES 2000

1-800-555-0000
CityBikes2000@yahoo.com
www.CityBikes2000.com

How to save 60% on bicycles and cycling equipment

Dear Customer,

CityBikes 2000 wants to help you save up to 60% on bicycles and cycling **paraphernalia**. We specialise in **refurbished** and **pre-owned name-brand** bikes including Schwinn, Cannondale and Atala.

Why pay full price for new bicycles when you can get beautiful refurbished bikes at up to 60% off?

As a full service dealer we have products and services to help you pick the right bike for your needs at a price you can afford. CityBikes 2000 is **networked** with **wholesalers** and **distributors** throughout the US to offer you an extensive range of bicycles and **gear** at a price that is **guaranteed** to fit your budget.

Please call us today at 1-800-555-0000 or visit us online at www.CityBikes2000.com. **Quote your exclusive promotional code MYBIKE and you'll receive a further 10% off your first order.**

We also buy used bicycles. If you have a bike you want to sell, we would love the opportunity to make a deal with you. For more information, please call us at 1-800-555-0000.

Best regards,

Josh Gray

MY GLOSSARY

paraphernalia	*n.*	（尤指某活动所需的）装备；大量用品
refurbish	*v.*	再装修；翻新
pre-owned	*adj.*	旧的；二手的
name-brand	*n.*	名牌；名牌货
networked	*adj.*	网络的；广播电视联播的

wholesaler	*n.*	批发商
distributor	*n.*	经销商，分销商
gear	*n.*	装备，装置；工具
guarantee	*v.*	保证；担保

4 Read the letter and answer these questions.

1) What are the products or services offered?

_____

2) What is the main offer?

_____

3) What further offer is there if you reply?

_____

4) How many times are their contact details and company name mentioned? Why do you think that is?

_____

5 Match the words with their definitions.

1) pick

2) afford

3) range

4) fit

5) budget

6) deal

a ☐ a business transaction or agreement

b ☐ to be suitable for a purpose or occasion

c ☐ a selection of goods of one particular type

d ☐ the amount of money you have available to spend

e ☐ to have enough money to pay for

f ☐ to choose or select from among a group

6 Use the expressions in the box to complete this unsolicited letter.

amazing offer	dynamic individual	friendly consultants	half the price
has selected you	incredibly low rate	now is the time	so why wait

Royal Gym Invites You to Get in Shape for Less

Dear Mr Pèrez,

(1) _____ to take care of yourself. You can't read a newspaper or watch a TV programme without learning yet another benefit of adding exercise to your daily routine. (2) _____?

Royal Gym (3) _____ for a year's membership at the (4) _____ of $ 40 a month, (5) _____ of a regular membership. Royal Gym offers a fitness centre with sauna yoga studio and juice bar.

Everything (6) _____ like you needs for modern living.

    Bring this letter with you when you come to speak with one of our (7) _____ to take advantage of this (8) _____!

Yours truly,

Lou Sherman
Royal Gym

Reading **3**

    Fliers can range from just a few key pieces of information to a couple of columns of text. No matter what style you choose, provide enough information so recipients realise the advantages of your product, **prompting** them to give you a call.

Let's get start. First, find a design software programme for making a flier, including Microsoft Word, which offers access to flier **templates** in which you **replace** the images and text with your own product.

Second, at the top of the page or in the right column, ask a question. Such a **headline** suggests how your services make your customers' lives easier.

Third, set up your flier with no columns or choose two columns to break up the information in easy-to-read segments. List services and **qualifications** and then follow the list of services with a sentence or two explaining your qualifications.

Fourth, toward the bottom of the page or the right column, add the name of your business or your own name. Immediately below your name, add your contact information. Include your phone number and email address. If you have a website for your business, include the link. Add an image or two to your flier, such as a picture of your product.

Before you print and hand out your newly designed flier, **proofread** it and ask someone else to give it a **thorough** reading to make sure it looks **professional**.

MY GLOSSARY

prompt	v.	促使; 导致; 激起
template	n.	样板; 模板
replace	v.	替换, 代替
headline	n.	(报纸的)大字标题
qualification	n.	资格; 学历; 素质; 技能

proofread	v.	校阅, 校对, 勘校
thorough	adj.	彻底的; 细致的
professional	adj.	职业的; 专业的

7 Read the text and choose the correct option.

1) What is a flier?

   A A flier includes a few key pieces of information or a couple of columns of text.

   B A flier provides information regarding a product or service, often with a special offer.

   C A flier lists services and qualifications.

2) Why do you set up your flier with no columns or two columns?

   A A design software programme for making a flier needs such a template.

   B In order to break up the information in easy-to-read segments.

   C In order to make a flier look professional.

3) In a flier, what kind of information do you have to mention?

   A A question suggesting how your services make your customers' lives easier.

   B An attractive headline.

C A few key pieces of information.

4) If you plan to make a flier, what is the most important thing?

A An attractive headline, services and qualifications.

B Contact details.

C All of the above.

5) Which of the following could be the title of the text?

A How to make a flier.

B The importance of making a flier.

C The style of a flier.

8 Match these sentences on the left with the functions on the right.

1) ☐ Why don't you give us a ring today?

2) ☐ How would you rate our website design?

3) ☐ Join our exclusive club now! You won't regret it.

4) ☐ Call us now for a free, no obligation quote.

5) ☐ Buy one, get one free!

6) ☐ Please tick the option which corresponds best to your view.

7) ☐ Act immediately. This could save you a fortune!

8) ☐ Bring this brochure with you and you'll get a fantastic free gift!

a Asking for an opinion

b Making an offer/promise

c Inviting someone to do something

d Persuading someone to do something

9 Translate the following sentences into Chinese.

1) This offer is limited to the first 50 customers.

_____

2) Don't miss this opportunity to save up to 40%.

_____

3) As a valued customer, we would like to offer you a special discount.

_____

4) You will be able to see all the advantages when you click on our website.

_____

5) Contact us within 15 days in order to claim your free gift.

_____

6) Thank you for your attention and we look forward to hearing from you soon.

_____

Writing

10 Complete the following unsolicited letter with the missing information in the box, changing the form if necessary.

> on our website
> receive your first order
> here at Pet Supermarket
>
> to give your pet a healthy and enjoyable life
> be pleased to offer you this exceptional deal

Dear Mrs/Mr Rowe,

We know you care about your pet and want to offer it the best at all times. For this reason we (1)_____ _____, valid for the next 7 days (2)_____ www.petsupermarket.com, 25% off for all pet food and toys. (3)_____, you can be sure of finding the best products, including grooming, toys and accessories, (4)_____.

We look forward to (5)_____ on www.petsupermarket.com or alternatively contact us at 800–125–125 to place your order over the phone.

Miranda Snow
Sales Manager
Pet Supermarket

Writing tips for unsolicited offers

- Grab the reader's attention with a strong opening statement, emphasising a discount or special offer for example.
- Make the reader feel special and personally selected, using expressions such as *only for you*, *specially selected*, *reserved* and *special customer*.
- Use imperatives and short sentences throughout the text so that the message is clear and effective.
- Underline the advantages / special offers / benefits that you offer by repeating the information in different ways.
- Mention your company name/website/address several times so that the reader will remember the details.
- Use lots of different fonts, capitals, bold type and exclamation marks to create an eye-catching letter.

Listening

11 **Mr Price from Pure Water calls Mrs O'Leary to promote his company's home water treatment system. Listen to their phone conversation and choose the correct option.**

1) Pure Water is offering _____.

    A a free trial of its product

    B seven free bottles of water to every household

    C seven families the chance to win its product

2) What does Mr Price think of bottled water?

    A It does not taste very good.

    B It is good quality.

    C It is expensive and bad for the environment.

3) Mr Price claims that his water treatment system _____.

    A will save Mrs O'Leary money

    B is easy to use

    C will make Mrs O'Leary happier

4) Why does Mr Price want an appointment?

    A To see Mrs O'Leary's home and family.

    B To test the water in Mrs O'Leary's home.

    C To show his product.

5) Mrs O'Leary's husband _____.

    A works for the same company as Mr Price

    B works for a local water authority

    C does not like telemarketers

12 **Complete the dialogue with the following sentences, and then listen to the recording to check your answers.**

Have you ever noticed	we have a special offer reserved for you	I'm not convinced
I often buy it	Just one more question	I'm not interested

Telemarketer: Good morning. My name is June Robbins and I'm calling from Carlo's. I'm pleased to tell you that (1) _____.

Customer: What kind of offer?

Telemarketer: Do you buy olive oil?

Customer: Well, yes. (2) _____.

Telemarketer: We offer a wonderful extra virgin olive oil delivered to your door directly from Italy.

Customer: I normally buy it in the supermarket. (3) _____, thank you.

Telemarketer: (4) _____. How much do you normally pay?

Customer: I can't really remember.

Telemarketer: (5) _____ that cheaper olive oils don't taste so good? Well, we can guarantee a superior product at a fraction of the supermarket prices. And you only need to purchase 8 bottles a month to be able to...

Customer: Sorry, (6) _____ by your offer. Goodbye.

Unsolicited Phone Calls

Telemarketer

- I'm pleased to tell you that you have been selected for...
- I can give you a no-obligation demonstration...
- Are you interested in saving money on your food/electricity / heating bills?
- Have you ever thought about...?
- Also don't forget that this will save you money.
- Just one more question...

Customer

- I'm not interested, thank you.
- Look, I have to go now.
- I've already said that I don't want to change/buy / know about it.
- I'd like to know more about your company/product.
- How much does it cost?
- What does it involve? / What do I have to do?

Speaking 2

13 **Practise this telemarketing phone call. Remember to swap roles.**

Telemarketer

You work for Frozy Foods, a company which sells frozen foods. You offer a wide selection of products, like vegetables, seafood, pizza, ready-made meals and ice cream. Clients can order by phone or Internet and delivery direct to the customer's door is within 24 hours, at an agreed time.

Customer

Use this information to decide how to respond to the telemarketing call you receive from Frozy Foods. You live alone in a small flat, with a tiny kitchen. You do not like cooking very much and prefer to eat out or get a take-away. Your nearest supermarket is 10 minutes away on foot. You have got Internet access.

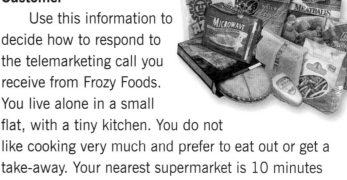

Thinking

14 **The following is an unsolicited inquiry letter. Could you summarise a format of an unsolicited inquiry letter? Learn and think.**

In business or in life, you have to make inquiries in case you want a new service or product or even help of someone. It is a formal letter where you don't know the receiver personally. This following letter is from Clarke Gable.

Dear Alec,

I am Clarke Gable, head of the sourcing department at Mahu Garments. We are looking for woven and knit fabrics required to make shirts and tops for both men and women. I have heard a

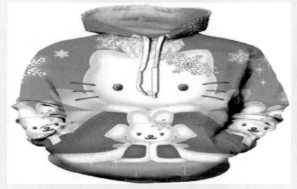

lot about your company's good fabric quality and good business ethics and would like to engage in business with you.

If it is possible, can you tell me the different types of fabrics you usually make along with their details like count, GSM and the finishes? If it's all right for you, I would like to visit your factory in near future to see your machines. Also, tell me the minimum order quantity and the price for the fabrics.

I look forward to your positive response and am privileged to be in business with you. Feel free to contact me at 27892 or my email id-clarke@gmail.com.

Thank You.

Regards,

Clarke Gable

Useful Expressions and Terms

unsolicited letter 不请自来的信件

unsolicited electronic message 不请自来的电子信息

introduce goods or services 介绍商品或服务

promotional offer 促销优惠

fill out a form 填写表格

make a purchase 购买

visit a website 访问网站

place a telephone call 打电话

fill up inboxes with spam 收件箱里塞满垃圾邮件

take up the various offers 接受各种各样的提议

cost-effective marketing method 合算的营销方法

strong persuasive language 具有很强说服力的语言

junk mail 垃圾邮件

phone directory 电话簿

behavioural characteristic 行为特征

wholesaler and distributor 批发商和分销商

exclusive promotional code 独家促销代码

make a deal with... 与……做交易

UNIT 5 Promotional Correspondence

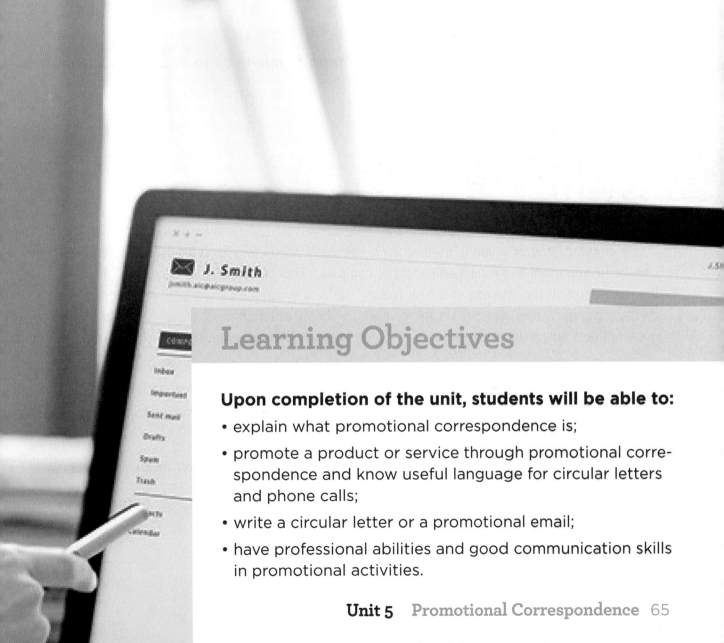

Learning Objectives

Upon completion of the unit, students will be able to:

- explain what promotional correspondence is;
- promote a product or service through promotional correspondence and know useful language for circular letters and phone calls;
- write a circular letter or a promotional email;
- have professional abilities and good communication skills in promotional activities.

Starting Off

How many emails do you receive promoting a product or a service? In fact, every email sent to a potential or current customer could be considered direct email marketing. Direct email marketing is a tool for building relationships with both existing and potential customers. There are two types of direct email marketing: direct email—it involves sending a promotional message in the form of an email, and it might be an announcement of a special offer; retention email—it usually takes the form of regular emails known as newsletters, which aim at developing a long-term impact on readers and contain information that informs, entertains or otherwise benefits them. Let's go on and explore more.

Speaking 1

1 **What kind of situation might a company need to inform all its customers about? Talk together.**

Reading 1

A **circular** letter or email is used when a company needs to inform all its customers about a change or important event happening in the company. This could be a new address, a change in the management, the opening of a new factory, store or e-commerce website. As they are sent to all the customers, new and old, on the company's database, circular letters also offer a marketing opportunity, a way of reminding clients of the company's services, products or benefits.

Circular letters can also be internal, sent to all staff within a company to inform them, for example, of changes in the **organisational** structure or various **administrative** matters.

> Tips for a circular letter or email:
> - Use mail-merge systems to **personalise** each letter with the customer's name.
> - Alternatively use *Dear Valued Customer* as an opening **salutation** instead of *Dear Sir/Madam.*
> - Make the letter personal by using *you*, rather than the **generic** *our customers.*
> - Be fairly brief and to the point.

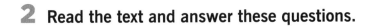

MY GLOSSARY

circular	*n.*	函件; 通告			主人的名字
organisational	*adj.*	组织的; 编制的	salutation	*n.*	称呼; 称呼语
administrative	*adj.*	管理的; 行政的	generic	*adj.*	通用的; 一般的, 普通的
personalise	*v.*	使个性化; 在……上标明			

2 Read the text and answer these questions.

1) Why do companies send circular letters?

   _____

2) Who are they sent to?

   _____

3) In what way are circular letters a marketing opportunity?

   _____

4) Are circular letters always sent to someone outside the company?

   _____

5) Why is it important to use the word *you* in a circular letter?

   _____

6) Why do you think a circular letter should be quite short?

   _____

3 Complete the letter below with the expressions from the box.

business relationship	customer service	recently appointed
the coming month	valuable asset	with pleasure

Dear Mr Gibbons,

It is (1) _____ that we inform you that we have (2) _____ Ms Ursula Grey as our sales representative for the South West region. She has worked in sales for over 10 years and I am sure she will be a (3) _____ to our company with her understanding of the sector and her excellent (4) _____ skills.

She will contact you in (5) _____ to introduce herself and show you the new samples from our autumn/winter collection.

We look forward to continuing our (6) _____ with you.

Yours sincerely,

Marjorie O'Brien

4 Match the two halves of the sentences.

1) We are pleased to announce that

    a ☐ to minimise any inconvenience during this time.

2) The steady growth of our business

    b ☐ will result in your orders being dealt with more promptly.

3) As our valued customer,

    c ☐ has made it necessary to relocate to larger premises.

4) This change in our sales team

    d ☐ we inform you of the retirement of our partner, Mr Guy Wood.

5) We will do our best

    e ☐ you will be entitled to a 15% discount for the first week.

6) It is with regret that

    f ☐ our new store will be opening in Shanghai on 2nd February.

Reading 2

Example of Circular Letter

Higgonson & Co.
21 West Way
Farnborough
GU14 9LP

Dear Valued Customer,

Due to the large increase in the volume of our trade with Germany, we have decided to open a **branch** in Frankfurt. Mr Dieter Beckermann, who has worked with us for the last 7 years, has been **appointed** as General Manager. This new branch will open on 1st September and from that date all orders and **enquiries** should be sent to:

Mr Dieter Beckermann
Higgonson & Co.
Stiftstrabe 25
D-60313 Frankfurt am Main
Tel: (+49) 69 0000123 Fax: (+49) 69 000012

We take this opportunity to express our thanks for your **custom** in the past and we are sure that this new branch will lead to even higher standards in the service we provide.
Yours faithfully,

Robin Wiley

European Director

MY GLOSSARY

branch	*n.* 分支机构; 分公司	
appoint	*v.* 任命; 委任	

enquiry	*n.* 询问; 打听	
custom	*n.* （顾客对商店的）惠顾, 光顾; 习俗	

USEFUL LANGUAGE

Circular Letters

Attracting attention

- Are you / your clients fed up with…?
- Have you ever wanted to try/experience/see…?
- As a long-standing and important customer of ours…
- We know you / your customers expect the best / are looking for something special.

Giving details

- We would like to draw your attention to…
- We are delighted to tell you about…
- It is with great pleasure that we announce…
- Dedicated to the younger members of the family, we have developed…

Referring to prices and special deals

- Bookings made before the end of the month qualify for a £250 discount.
- There are several pricing options available to satisfy all your customers.
- As one of our valued customers, we are delighted to offer you a 10% discount.
- This special introductory offer is available until 30th June.

5 Read the circular letter and answer these questions.

1) What is the purpose of the letter?

_____

2) Who is Mr Dieter Beckermann?

_____

3) What should German customers do from 1st September?

_____

4) What assurance does Mr Wiley give the customers?

_____

6 Fill in the blanks with words or expressions from the box, changing the form if necessary.

fed up with	qualify for	generic	salutation
dedicated to	valued customer	circular	administrative

1) These workers are _____ being at the bottom of the pile when it comes to pay.

2) This conference will be _____ the research of the eco development of enterprises.

3) These companies improved their financial performance enough to _____ the Forbes Global 2000.

4) He mailed the _____ to all subscribers this morning.

5) Use a(n) _____ such as *Dear Mr Smith* in a header. This will make you professional in your clients' mind.

6) Other industries have had to sack managers to reduce _____ costs.

7) Our aim and principle is to offer the best quality products and services to every _____.

8) This index at the back of the book lists both brand and _____ names.

Writing

7 Write a circular letter to inform your customers of your new company address. Include the following points:

- you will move on the 1st of next month;
- telephone, fax numbers and email addresses will not change;
- the move is due to the expansion of the company;
- apologise for any disruption to business during the move.

8 Suppose you own a shop selling smartphones and accessaries. Write a short circular letter to your clients to inform them that you have set up a website and now offer online sales. Invite them to visit the site and take advantage of your special offer.

Listening

Another way to promote a product or service is on the phone. The advantages of making a phone call are that it is immediate and you have instant feedback that you can follow up on for the future. On the other hand, a promotional phone call can be a disruption while someone is working and may feel intrusive if the caller is too insistent.

9 You will hear a promotional phone call between a tour operator and a travel agent. Listen to the conversation and decide whether these sentences are true (*T*) or false (*F*).

	T	F
1) Rob and Tanya don't know each other.	☐	☐
2) Tanya is promoting tours to Rob.	☐	☐
3) Rob isn't interested in what Tanya offers him.	☐	☐
4) Tanya is happy at the end of the conversation.	☐	☐

10 Listen again and complete these sentences. Then match them to the functions they express.

1) _____ I'm calling is to tell you about our new season's tours.

2) Great! What have you got _____?

3) It _____ sightseeing of the city, a cruise of the Biscayne Bay and an Everglades Airboat Ride.

4) It sounds good—can you _____ the details?

5) That _____ expensive...

6) I _____ everything to you today so you can look at all the information...

a ☐ giving reason for calling

b ☐ expressing doubt

c ☐ providing details

d ☐ requesting more information

e ☐ promising action

f ☐ showing interest

USEFUL LANGUAGE

Promotional Phone Calls

Introducing the reason for the call
- I know your clients are interested in...so I'd like to propose...
- I remember that you deal with / organise/do a lot of business with...so I wanted to tell you about...
- I believe you will be interested in our new offer.

Highlighting the selling point/Convincing
- Another excellent/unique aspect is...
- Don't forget that we also include a free...
- What makes this special/different/excellent / value for money / appealing is that...

Asking questions about the product/service
- What makes your deal different?
- What does it include?
- Why should I change to using your services?
- How is it better than what I already offer?

Promising action
- I'll pop some leaflets in the post for you.
- I'll send you all the details by email.
- I'll call you back to arrange a meeting.

Dear **Survivalists**,

There's a HUGE difference between interest and **commitment**. When you're interested, you do what is convenient. But, when you are **committed**, you do what is necessary.

Survivalists don't take things for granted. They want to prepare for their family.
http://survivallife.com/committed-to-survival

And until Midnignt Tonight, you can get the entire **deck** FOR FREE.

I Am Committed To My Survival.

Now I ask…
Are you simply interested?
Or are you committed?

I wanted to make this offer as easy and **affordable** as possible. And nothing is easier than FREE! But this offer is all over Tonight at Midnight.

Click here to get your pack while supplies last!
Remember, we're all in this together!

"Above Average" Joe

P.S. I'm committed to you getting these playing cards, but you must act now! I only have a few decks in stock and I don't want you to miss out on this offer!
http://survivallife.com/committed-to-survival

Revolution Golf Training Aids
To: Scott Martin
How to FEEL the perfect golf swing

Hi Scott Martin,

Our friend Martin Chuck has invented something new…to help you "feel" a bulletproof swing. Click the image below to discover more.

It's a ball you place between your arms.
Yes—it sounds a little crazy but it's working. Martin's students love it.

survivalist	n.	求生训练学员, 户外生存受训者
commitment	n.	（对工作或某活动）献身, 奉献, 投入
commit	v.	承诺; 致力于
deck	n.	一副纸牌
affordable	adj.	便宜的; 价格合理的; 负担得起的

11 Read the two emails and answer these questions.

1) What is the purpose of the first email?

_____

2) How to make the call to action crystal clear?

_____

3) Could you find the differences between the two emails?

_____

4) How does the first email restate the offer and communicate scarcity?

_____

5) What is a promotional email made up of from the two emails?

_____

12 Complete the promotional letter with the sentences in the box.

we have recently launched a new scheme	we are in the IT business
we had recently met	I am sending you a brochure of models
I look forward to your response	we can fix a formal meeting
our company has a team of professionals	I am sure you must have liked the offer

Dear Mr Amira,

(1) _____ at a Technology Expo held at Texas University. There you had spoken about having advanced PCs in your workshop and that you were looking to sell them and buy new PCs. Our company, as I had told you, deals in all types of computer systems and peripherals.

(2) _____ "Exchange for New", wherein you can exchange your old working systems for new up-to-date systems at a nominal fee. (3) _____ for 10 years and are known for providing quality services, both sales and after sales. (4) _____ who can check and pick up old systems from your home at no extra cost.

(5) _____ we are offering. There is also another offer—"For every

purchase of 10 systems, you get a coloured laser printer at no extra cost." You will not find any such offer and such competitive price anywhere.

(6) _____ and by the end of the letter you would have made up your mind. (7) _____ . Then (8) _____ and discuss all the things in detail.

Waiting for your reply.

Yours truly,

Liza Kudrow

Sales Manager

Speaking 2

13 In pairs, read the situation and act out the phone conversation. Sit back-to-back so you can't see your partner's face to make it more realistic. Remember to swap roles.

Promoter

You work for a company which organises food and cultural holidays in your country and you want to promote a new holiday to UK travel agents. The holiday is 7 days, half-board, with flights from Heathrow and Gatwick airports. You can invent the details, such as a cookery course, visit to a castle or famous monument and the price.

Travel agent

You are a travel agent in the UK and receive a phone call from a company promoting a new food and cultural holiday. Depending on what information the caller gives you, ask about the activities, the size of the group, the target market and the price. You can choose to request further information, for example by email, or to politely tell the caller you are not interested.

14 **The following is an email ad. Do you think it is a successful ad? How about the call to action in the email ad? Learn and think.**

De Beers made its call-to-action button stand out in three ways. First, the CTA was created in a colour that complimented the email's design but stood out from it (in this case, light blue). Second, to speak to women planning their big day, they formed an immediate wedding connection with the "Discover Your Bridal Style" text on an unusually oversized CTA that attracts real attention. Third, to make diamond jewellery closely connected with wedding, key words are repeated many times, such as *bridal style*, *personal style* and *bridal inspiration*.

DE BEERS
JEWELLERY

WEDDING BANDS | ENGAGEMENT RINGS | BRIDAL INSPIRATION

WHAT IS YOUR BRIDAL STYLE?

If you or a friend are getting married, or if you are simply dreaming of your future nuptials, allow us to inspire you with everything from exquisite bouquets to sparkling diamond jewellery and dream dresses that perfectly complement your personal style.

DISCOVER YOUR BRIDAL STYLE

Useful Expressions and Terms

promotional correspondence 促销信件

circular letter 通告信; 通知书

mail-merge system 邮件合并系统

valued customer 重要客户

opening salutation 开场问候

open a branch 设立分公司

take this opportunity 利用这次机会

valuable asset 宝贵财富

be fed up with 对……感到厌烦

long-standing and important customer 长期和重要的客户

be dedicated to 从事; 致力于

special deal 优惠促销

qualify for 有……的资格

follow up on instant feedback 跟踪及时反馈

promising action 有可能的行动

pop some leaflets 放置一些传单

in the post 在邮件中

travel agent 旅行代理商

in stock 有存货

miss out on this offer 错过这次优惠

ELEVATE YOUR JOB SEARC

Apply at totaljob

Learning Objectives

Upon completion of the unit, students will be able to:

- know the elements of advertising, the historical events in the development of advertising and how to create an effective advert;
- analyse a long-standing logo, slogan or advert;
- write an essay or report on advertising;
- have professional abilities and good communication skills in advertising.

Starting Off

As we live in an information age, we have to live with advertising messages no matter whether we like them or not. Advertising is a component of marketing. Marketing is the broad process of researching consumer needs. Advertising, on the other hand, strictly refers to the process of reaching potential customers in an effort to make sales. Businesses have the opportunity to choose from several advertising types, including print advertising, broadcast advertising, digital advertising and outdoor advertising. While each of these types presents its own pros, a savvy advertiser chooses the one type or the combination of types that best suits the company's product, target consumers and advertising budget. Let's go on and explore more.

Reading 1

Advertising is perhaps the most important aspect of promotion, the fourth P in the marketing mix, and is used to **persuade**, **inform** and remind. It can persuade consumers to buy or use an existing product or service; it can inform them about changes within a company or a new product or service; it can remind them about a company, thus improving its image and building brand identity.

Companies generally divide their advertising into two distinct areas:

- Business-to-consumer (B2C) advertising: to persuade the general public to buy the company's products or use its services.

- Business-to-business (B2B) advertising: directed at other businesses to inform them about the company and to promote its products and services.

The first thing an advertisement has to do is to grab our attention and it can achieve this in a variety of ways: a **slogan**, a **striking** image, a **catchy jingle** or a memorable headline. The second thing is to provide more information about the product or service. In a print ad, this will be the body of the ad. The purpose is to create feelings of belief, trust and desire. The third aspect is to make sure that potential customers can remember the company or product and to reinforce the brand identity, for example with the logo. The final element, the call to action, may be **implicit** within the ad or specified **explicitly**, such as inviting viewers to click on a website or visit a store.

Since we are surrounded by advertising in all aspects of our lives, we are perhaps becoming more resistant and less open to it. Therefore agencies and ad designers have to try to make their ad stand out in a crowd and new advertising models are continuously developed and new media options are explored so as to continue to reach the target audience.

1 **Read the text and answer these questions.**

1) What is the purpose of advertising?

_____

2) What is the difference between B2B and B2C advertising?

_____

3) What are the five things that an advert should do?

_____

4) How can an advert catch our attention?

_____

5) How does an advert try to make us remember a product or company?

_____

6) Do you believe that consumers today are more resistant to advertising? Why / Why not?

_____

2 **Match each element of an advert with the correct definition.**

1) slogan   **a** ☐ the photograph, pictures or other visual elements in an advert

2) image   **b** ☐ the main text of a print ad, with information on the product or service

3) jingle   **c** ☐ a short, well thought-out sentence, usually the first part of a print ad to be read

4) headline   **d** ☐ the unique symbol used by a company or brand

5) body   **e** ☐ a memorable tune or piece of music, mostly used in radio commercials

6) logo   **f** ☐ a short, catchy and distinctive phrase to describe a product or a brand

3 Match these functions with the sentences.

1) Make the viewer take a specific action now.

    a ☐ *Start your trial* or *Click here* or *Book now* or *Buy now*.

2) Educate consumers about specific products and services.

    b ☐ Let consumers know that a retailer carries a specific product and that they can go there to purchase it.

3) Influence consumer behaviour.

    c ☐ At a specific store, they can buy designer clothing for half the price they would pay at other retailers.

4) Make shopping easier.

    d ☐ Demonstrate how the product works and how it can solve the problems they face.

5) Communicate price and value.

    e ☐ Mention a money-back guarantee or offer a free trial.

Reading 2

Effective Advertising

When creating an advert and defining an advertising campaign, most businesses use the services of an advertising agency. Here specialists follow all aspects from the definition of the USP (unique selling **proposition**) and the creation of the ad, to the selection of the advertising media and the length and timing of the campaign.

When creating an ad, agencies and ad designers can try to achieve the objectives of a successful advert—that it should be noticed, read, believed, remembered and acted upon—in different ways. They can use a traditional approach or try to be more original. Both of these have advantages as well as potential **drawbacks**.

Traditional language, images and associations have been tried and tested and are known to work. On the other hand, random or unconnected images, **bizarre** headlines or invented words can be considered **groundbreaking** and modern. The **downsides** are that the first approach may just seem boring and over-used; the second could be too **obscure** to be properly understood or to catch on.

Humour is another common technique and it is often considered the most successful by consumers and agencies alike, as a funny or entertaining ad is more likely to be remembered.

The use of famous people as **testimonials** can also be considered. A famous actor, sportsperson or model has a very powerful personal image and can bring this to the advert. However, it can be an extremely expensive option and public opinion about who is in or cool can change very fast. **Gossip** and **scandals surrounding** a **celebrity** also risk damaging the company's image.

USP stands for unique selling proposition and is what differentiates a company's products or services from the rest of the competition.

A critical part of promotion and advertising, the USP conveys the real or **perceived** benefit of a product or service as a way to convince buyers to prefer one brand/company over another.

MY GLOSSARY

proposition	*n.*	提议; 建议	testimonial	*n.*	证明信; 介绍信; 推荐信
drawback	*n.*	缺点; 不利条件			
bizarre	*adj.*	极其怪诞的; 异乎寻常的	gossip	*n.*	流言蜚语, 闲言碎语
groundbreaking	*adj.*	开创性的; 创新的	scandal	*n.*	丑事, 丑闻
downside	*n.*	缺点; 不利方面	surround	*v.*	与……紧密相关; 围绕
obscure	*adj.*	费解的, 难以理解的	celebrity	*n.*	名人; 名流
humour	*n.*	幽默; 诙谐	perceived	*adj.*	感知到的; 感观的

4 **Read the text and decide if these sentences are true (*T*) or false (*F*). If there is not enough information, choose "doesn't say" (*DS*).**

	T	F	DS
1) Advertising agencies only follow big clients.	☐	☐	☐
2) Advertising agencies' services are limited to the creative aspect of an ad.	☐	☐	☐
3) A traditional approach to creating an ad does not have any disadvantages.	☐	☐	☐
4) An original ad may contain strange or made-up words.	☐	☐	☐
5) Both consumers and agencies believe humorous ads to be successful.	☐	☐	☐
6) The use of famous people in ad campaigns is in decline.	☐	☐	☐

5 Find the synonyms for the following words in the text.

1) assistance   _____

2) choice   _____

3) duration   _____

4) goals   _____

5) benefits   _____

6) disadvantages   _____

7) method   _____

8) jeopardise   _____

6 Fill in the blanks with words from the box, changing the form if necessary.

humour	perceived	persuade	information
slogan	desire	advertisement	proposition

1) Advertising is the transmission of information. Sometimes the information contained in the _____ is clear, direct and obvious. Advertisers broadcast information to some audience through sound, texts, or images.

2) Different kinds of price promotion have a significantly positive effect on consumer's _____ benefit of sales promotion.

3) Leaflets are a direct and cost-efficient way of getting _____ to large numbers of people. Information commonly found on a leaflet includes phone numbers, addresses, special promotions and coupons.

4) _____ in advertising has always been a good strategy for getting attention, delivering a message and making it memorable.

5) Advertising is a non-personal communication of information that is usually designed to win consumers through _____.

6) The function of a(n) _____ is to get across a brand's identity in a way that positions the brand in the minds of consumers.

7) Advertisements give answers to a consumer's questions, including where to eat, where to go, or what to buy. Effective advertising works to create a(n) _____ while offering an attractive solution.

8) The unique selling _____ is a marketing concept first proposed as a theory to explain a pattern in successful advertising campaigns of the early 1940s.

7 Listen to this manager from an advertising agency talking about creating an effective ad and complete the notes.

Step 1 — have a clear _____ so your message is focused.

Step 2 — understand the _____ of your ad to make it appropriate and produce results.

Step 3 — show how your product or service will _____ a consumer.

Step 4 — know your USP to define your _____ _____ and use it in your advert.

Step 5 — _____ with the customer, be motivating and encouraging but always believable.

8 Listen again and decide if these sentences are true (*T*) or false (*F*).

	T	F
1) An increase in sales is an example of what results a company might want from an advert.	☐	☐
2) The target of an ad is always the end user of a product.	☐	☐
3) Market research carried out in advance by the company will help define its target market.	☐	☐
4) Customers want to see the immediate benefits in order to buy a product or service.	☐	☐
5) Words and images cannot be used to motivate and engage consumers.	☐	☐
6) The longer and more complicated an ad, the better it will be remembered.	☐	☐

Speaking 1

9 **Discuss the following questions about ads in pairs.**

1) How many advertisements do you come into contact with in a day? Where are they?

2) How many advertisements do you remember well?

3) Are the ads you remembered more traditional or innovative? In what ways?

4) Do the ads use any humour? If so, do you think it is entertaining or funny?

5) Do the ads feature a famous person? Who? What ideas do you associate with him/her?

6) In general, which of the above-mentioned techniques do you prefer in an ad? Why?

Writing 1

10 **The following is a short essay explaining the purpose of advertising and how to make it appealing and effective. Complete the missing information with words or expressions from the box, changing the form if necessary.**

better convince us to buy a product	persuade us to change our behaviour
repetition association	inform us about products and services
advertising agents try to be more original	humour

    Nowadays, advertising has become a part of life. Some of us like it while others may hate it, but none of us can avoid it. Advertising not only (1)_____ but also (2)_____. Advertisers or (3)_____ use a variety of techniques in order to (4)_____, to shape our attitude towards their products. They may use a traditional approach or (5)_____. These techniques may include (6)_____, the use of famous people as testimonials, (7)_____, vague terms, emotional appeal, and (8)_____.

Speaking 2

11 **Choose one of these statements to support. Then have a class debate.**

> Consumers are able to make their own decisions and are not influenced by advertising.

> Advertising brainwashes people into buying things they do not want or need.

Think about:

- the amount of advertising we see/hear every day;
- financial investment in advertising;
- rational, independent decision making;
- today's consumer society;
- the difference between a real need and a want;
- following trends and being part of a group;
- advertising aimed at children.

Reading

A

Over time, advertising has had to respond to changes in cultural context, business demands and technology. While word-of-mouth advertising has probably existed since man first began to trade and sell goods and services, the forms of advertising we know today came about thanks to the development of the printing press and the expansion of newspapers. Paid advertisements started appearing in newspapers in the 17th century. They were quite simple, with lots of informative rather than persuasive texts, and were used to announce things like the publication of a new book or the performance of a play, as well as for personal ads like "lost and found".

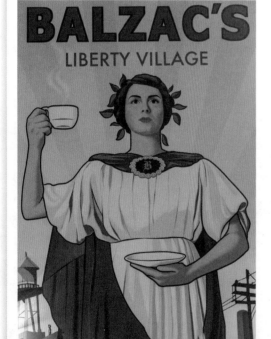

B

With the Industrial Revolution manufacturers were able to produce more goods in less time and were no longer restricted to local markets. They needed to persuade consumers all over the country—and sometimes in other parts of the world—about the benefits of their products compared with those of their competitors. Newspapers, which had become cheaper and more widely available, were the perfect way to reach this mass market of potential customers. These first advertisements just had simple descriptions of the products, with the price. By the mid-19th century it was possible to add **illustrations**. The language changed too and became more persuasive. And by the late 19th century, as manufacturers faced increased competition and began to understand the importance of advertising in getting their products known and sold, the first advertising agencies were set up. They offered the services of **illustrators** and **copywriters** to produce specifically designed adverts. They began to research the company and product, as well as the target market, and also started to monitor sales in relation to advertising campaigns.

C ⬜

Posters and outdoor advertising were more common in Europe than in the USA, but with the **outbreak** of World War I many countries started to use posters as **propaganda**—a way to **enforce** government policies and to get men to **enlist** to fight against the enemy. These posters often used **psychological manipulation** to frighten or **shame** the audience. With cinema and radio, there were new ways for advertising to reach a mass audience and the idea of creating a need in the consumer began to **dominate** advertising in the 1920s. The Great Depression negatively affected advertising spend, so advertising got tougher. It started to use key ideas such as the desire to belong, **subconscious** fears and sex appeal, marketing products as necessities rather than **luxuries**.

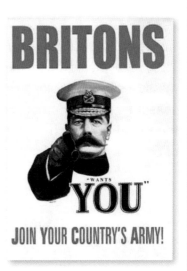

D ⬜

Post-war **affluence**, a **boom** in consumer spending and the perfect way to reach a mass audience—television— all meant an increase in advertising in the 1950s. At first companies **sponsored**, and even produced, TV programmes, then television started to offer the commercial breaks we still have today between programmes. Madison Avenue in New York became the centre of the US advertising business, and working in advertising was a well-paid and powerful profession, particularly for men. David Ogilvy, for example, set up a world-class advertising agency and introduced many ideas which are still part of advertising practice today. The same period, however, also saw Vance Packard accuse the advertising industry of using hidden techniques to **manipulate** and brainwash the public.

E ⬜

As the 20th century started to near its end, the competition in advertising became fiercer, with bigger and bigger agencies dealing with larger and larger clients, budgets and markets. The arrival of the Internet and World Wide Web, with endless opportunities for **pop-up** and **banner** advertising, caused a big shake up in the advertising world, as did targeted ads, social marketing and **viral** ad campaigns. A lot of advertising spend moved from traditional media to digital media, in order to keep up with the changes in business and consumer demand.

The book *The Hidden Persuaders* by Vance Packard was published in 1957. It explores the theme of psychological manipulation and **subliminal** messages in advertising to influence the public, create a desire and **compel** consumers to buy products that they do not want or need. It questions the **morality** of such techniques and also looks at their use in the world of politics.

MY GLOSSARY

illustration	*n.*	图表; 插图
illustrator	*n.*	插图画家
copywriter	*n.*	广告文字撰写人
poster	*n.*	招贴画; 海报
outbreak	*n.*	爆发; （疾病）突然发生
propaganda	*n.*	宣传; 宣传机构
enforce	*v.*	强制执行, 强行实施
enlist	*v.*	入伍; 征募; 从军
psychological	*adj.*	心理的; 精神上的
manipulation	*n.*	操纵, 操作; 处理
shame	*v.*	使羞愧, 使惭愧
dominate	*v.*	控制, 支配
subconscious	*adj.*	下意识的, 潜意识的
luxury	*n.*	奢侈品
affluence	*n.*	富裕; 丰富
boom	*n.*	（贸易和经济活动的）激增, 繁荣
sponsor	*v.*	赞助（活动、节目等）
manipulate	*v.*	（暗中）控制, 操纵; 影响
pop-up	*adj.*	有弹出功能的; 能迅速显示的
banner	*n.*	横幅图片的广告模式; 横幅
viral	*adj.*	病毒的; 病毒性的
subliminal	*adj.*	下意识的, 潜意识的
compel	*v.*	强迫, 迫使
morality	*n.*	道德; 道德准则

12 Read the text quickly and match these titles to the correct paragraphs.

Ad Men	Propaganda and Persuasion	Newspaper Advertising
The Digital Age	The Industrial Revolution	

13 Read the text again and answer these questions.

1) What were newspaper ads like in the 17th century?

_____

2) How did newspaper ads change during the 19th century?

_____

3) What services did the first advertising agencies offer their clients?

_____

4) What was often the subject of advertising during World War I?

_____

5) How did advertising change in the 1920s and 1930s?

_____

6) What led to an increase in advertising in the 1950s?

_____

7) What was the importance of Madison Avenue to the advertising industry?

_____

8) What happened to advertising expenditure because of digital media?

_____

14 **Match these words from the text with the correct definitions.**

1) word-of-mouth   **a** ☐   to make people believe something by constantly telling them it is true and preventing access to other information

2) persuasive   **b** ☐   making someone want to do or believe something

3) propaganda   **c** ☐   never finishing, or appearing never to finish

4) boom   **d** ☐   information, often one-sided, spread with the aim of influencing public opinion

5) brainwash   **e** ☐   an increase in something

6) endless   **f** ☐   through people telling people about something

Writing 2

15 **Find out about an international or national logo, slogan or advertising campaign that has stood the test of time. Write a short report answering these questions.**

- Who created it?
- What is it like?
- How long has it been used?
- How much has it changed over the years?
- Why do you think it continues to be successful?

Thinking

16 **The following is Coca-Cola's brand naming localisation strategy. What's the purpose of the multinational corporation? Learn and think.**

A good brand name can help a product win a universal praise. Coca-Cola's Chinese brand name emerged victoriously in various global markets. Because of this translated name *Kekou Kele*, which was accepted by Chinese consumers, Coca-Cola got a great success in Chinese marketing.

A brand name which can be suitable for reading aloud is the sound part of the brand. It is also the key element and the most distinctive feature of the brand as well as the basic form of brand culture concept. A good brand name itself is one of the simplest and the most direct advertising language. It can quickly and effectively express the central contents of this company. From this view, *Kekou Kele* is a good example.

"Coca" and "Cola" stand for two primary ingredients in English. The Chinese name of Coca-Cola doesn't have this meaning; however, *Kekou Kele* became another creation. *Kekou*, an adjective in Chinese, is often used to describe delicious food, so *Kekou* will make consumers naturally feel that the product is flavourful. *Kele* is completely an

innovative idea which hadn't been used in China until the translator put it up. As soon as Chinese people refer to *le*, it will be associated with *kuaile*—meaning *happy* in Chinese. That's why *Kekou Kele* was accepted by Chinese people immediately. In other words, this localised brand name fits the cultural psychology of ordinary Chinese people. Brand naming localisation is a great tool for a multinational corporation to promote its brand.

Useful Expressions and Terms

business-to-consumer (B2C) 企业对消费者的电子商务模式

business-to-business (B2B) 企业对企业的电子商务模式

catchy jingle 吸引人的旋律

the body of the ad 广告主体

reinforce the brand identity 强化品牌识别

call to action 呼吁行动

develop advertising models 开发广告模式

explore new media options 探索新的媒体选择

advertising agency 广告代理商

the USP (unique selling proposition) 独特的销售主张

act upon 对……起作用

catch on 理解, 明白; 变得流行

word-of-mouth advertising 口头广告

printing press 印刷术

paid advertisement 付费广告

personal ad 个人广告

lost and found 失物招领

simple description of the product 产品的简单描述

outdoor advertising 户外广告

create a need in the customer 在客户中创造一种需求

the Great Depression 大萧条

the desire to belong 渴望归属感

subconscious fear 潜意识里的恐惧

commercial break 商业广告时段

World Wide Web 万维网

banner advertising 横幅广告

big shake up 巨大的震动

in the advertising world 在广告界

targeted ad 定向广告

viral ad campaign 病毒式广告

UNIT
7 Advertising Media

Learning Objectives

Upon completion of the unit, students will be able to:

- understand the advantages and disadvantages of different advertising media and explain the factors that affect the choice of media for advertising campaigns;
- apply the most appropriate mix of media to advertise some products and services;
- analyse TV/radio commercials and write a report;
- have professional abilities and good communication skills in the choice of advertising media mix.

Starting Off

We are living in an environment with various advertising messages. Selection of the media outlet through which an ad will be presented has important implications for the success of a promotion. Each outlet possesses unique characteristics, though not all outlets are equally effective for all advertisers. Today's marketers must be well-versed in a wide range of media options. The reason for the growing number of media outlets is the advances in communication technology, including the continued growth in importance of the Internet and wireless communication. This is changing how consumers and businesses are responding to advertising messages. Let's go on and explore more.

Reading 1

The choice of the media for an advertising campaign depends on several factors, including:

- size, nature and location of the target market;
- the product or service to be promoted;
- what **proportion** of the **target** audience will be exposed to the ad;
- the cost.

Press

The press has a leading role in advertising campaigns. Printed adverts have the advantage that they can be kept, are often seen repeatedly and can contain more information or details than a TV ad. Their visual **impact** is still great even without sound or movement. Depending on the target, in an ad campaign it is possible to include international, national and regional newspapers (often a specific **section** like business, sport or fashion) and general interest or special interest magazines (e.g. computer, sport, hobbies). Naturally, a full colour ad in a **glossy** magazine is more expensive, and reaches a larger audience, than a black and white ad at the back of a local newspaper.

In order to promote their services or products, B2B advertisers use the trade press—magazines and other **publications** focusing on specific trades or industries—in order to be able to reach the correct audience and decision makers in a cost-efficient manner.

TV

This is still one of the most popular choices given its high impact and wide national reach. It is effective for creating brand **awareness** and selling consumer products. However, with the large number of satellite and cable TV channels now available, it is no longer **sufficient** to advertise just on the top three or four networks, but it is essential to choose the channel and programme

with the specific demographic required. TV advertising is extremely expensive, especially for the prime time **slots** such as early evening or during sporting events, and similarly the investment needed to produce the ad itself is huge. Another downside to TV advertising is that new digital technology allows viewers to skip adverts during **playback** or viewing, or viewers may just take a break or channel **hop** during the **commercial** breaks.

Radio

This is a cheaper **alternative** to TV advertising, both to purchase the **airtime** and to make the ad. It can be national or local but does not reach the same number of people as TV. The creation of the ad has to be carefully considered as it cannot rely on the impact of visual images.

Outdoor

Outdoor advertising includes **billboards**, posters, street furniture and electric signs in public places such as the street, shopping centres, airports, stations and on public transport. Some are

much more **permanent** and have become almost part of the background, while others are changed more frequently, such as on public transport, to maintain impact. The target is the general public, although the location, for example in a football stadium or near a school, can target a more specific market **segment**.

Digital Media

The most rapidly growing sector, Internet, offers targeted advertising worldwide 24/7 with banners, pop-up ads, and pay per click advertising, as well as one-to-one emails. Digital advertising is relatively inexpensive, can use sound, visuals and motion to create impact and it is easy to update and **evaluate** the success rate. A disadvantage is that these ads are very easy for users to ignore while surfing and to delete from their inbox. With social media and apps, advertisers are able to form a more direct contact with consumers, especially young people, creating a global community around a brand or product with consequent positive effects on sales and brand identity. Another advantage of social media is how **swiftly** messages can be spread. Viral ads, for example, can be posted on YouTube or Facebook where they are noticed by net surfers and shared immediately, quickly reaching millions of hits.

There are various organisations, such as the Advertising Standards Authority (ASA) in the UK, which regulate all forms of advertising and check advertisers' **compliance** with the rules. For example, there are certain products like tobacco and alcohol which cannot be advertised close to schools.

It is essential to find the right media mix in order to be sure that the campaign is as successful as possible and the advertising budget is well spent. The incredible growth of digital media and its huge potential means that companies need to find the right mix of traditional and digital media to stay ahead of the competition and keep in touch with consumers. In conclusion, if a consumer is engaged with an ad, he or she is more likely to buy the product or service.

MY GLOSSARY

proportion	n.	份额; 部分
target	n.	目标; 对象
impact	n.	巨大影响; 强大作用
section	n.	部分; 节; 段
glossy	adj.	光彩夺目的; 有光泽的
publication	n.	（书刊等的）出版, 发行
awareness	n.	意识; 认识; 兴趣
sufficient	adj.	足够的; 充足的
slot	n.	时段
playback	n.	录音（或录像、电话留言等的）回放
hop	n.	换来换去; 不断更换
commercial	n.	商业广告; adj. 商业的; 贸易的
alternative	n.	可供选择的事物
airtime	n.	（广播或电视节目的）播放时间
billboard	n.	公告牌; 告示牌; 广告牌
permanent	adj.	永恒的; 长久的
segment	n.	部分; 段
evaluate	v.	评价; 评估
compliance	n.	服从, 顺从, 遵从
swiftly	adv.	很快地; 即刻

1 Read the text and complete the table.

Advertising Media	Advantages	Disadvantages
press		
TV		
radio		
outdoor		
digital media		

2 Which advertising media do these terms refer to? Write a definition for each term.

1) prime time slot   *TV*   *space in a TV programme during early evening or during sporting events*

2) channel hopping   _____   _____

3) glossy magazine   _____   _____

4) trade press   _____   _____

5) billboard   _____   _____

6) street furniture   _____   _____

7) banner   _____   _____

8) pop-up ad   _____   _____

3 Translate the following expressions into Chinese.

1) advertising media   _____

2) an advertising campaign   _____

3) the commercial breaks   _____

4) brand identity   _____

5) the trade press   _____

6) a cost-efficient manner   _____

7) brand awareness   _____

8) the prime time slots   _____

4 Fill in the blanks with words from the box, changing the form if necessary.

| publication | commercial | target | alternative |
| awareness | billboard | click | evaluate |

1) The government has decided that the _____ of the report would be contrary to the public interest.

2) The money will be used to regenerate the _____ heart of the town.

3) Young people are a prime _____ group for marketing strategies.

4) The _____ will be funded by 100 sponsors, including 40 premier sponsors.

5) The campaign is intended to raise public _____ of protecting our Earth.

6) If you've forgotten your login ID, _____ this link.

7) We should invest in clean, _____ sources of energy, like advanced biofuels and natural gas.

8) The market situation is difficult to _____.

Speaking 1

5 In small groups, discuss which media or mix of media would be most appropriate to advertise these products and services.

- a shampoo available in supermarkets
- a low-cost dental surgery in your town
- a local repair service for electrical appliances
- cruise holidays in the Caribbean
- a website selling children's toys
- an energy drink

Reading 2

Leaflets and Brochures

Promotional materials like **leaflets** and brochures can be printed and distributed to customers or made available online or on apps. As they are a form of advertising, the language used in both leaflets and brochures needs to be promotional and persuasive. In the tourism industry, for instance, readers are drawn in and can imagine themselves on the holiday or visiting a particular place.

Leaflet

A leaflet is a piece of paper, often A4 size, **folded** into three and printed on both sides in colour, used to promote a company's products or services. They are particular common in the tourist sector where they promote towns, tourist attractions, guided tours and trips. They can be found in the **reception** areas of a company, train stations, tourist information centres and hotel lobbies. There is usually a short introduction or descriptive text and a selection of photos. To help the reader decide if the product or service is suitable for them, a leaflet should include practical information such as location, a map, facilities, opening times, prices and contact details.

Brochure

A brochure is a glossy **booklet** of many pages used to provide more detailed information on a company and its services or products. There is usually an introduction to the company, maybe with its history, experience and business **ethics**. Brochures are widely used in the tourism industry to promote holidays and can be handed out in travel agencies or **consulted** online. They contain descriptions of the destinations, hotels, **resorts** or **cruises**, **illustrated** with beautiful photography of the locations, rooms, facilities and so on. There is also information regarding prices, dates and the terms and conditions.

MY GLOSSARY

leaflet	n.	散页印刷品; 传单; 小册子
fold	v.	折叠, 对折（纸、织物等）
reception	n.	接待处; 接待区
booklet	n.	小册子
ethics	n.	行为准则; 道德原则

consult	v.	咨询; 请教
resort	n.	旅游胜地; 度假胜地
cruise	n.	乘船游览; 航行
illustrate	v.	加插图于; 给（书等）做图表

6 Read the text and answer these questions.

1) What do leaflets often promote?

_____

2) Why should they contain practical information?

_____

3) Where can you find brochures?

_____

4) What are the main features of a brochure?

_____

7 Complete the mind map with the types of promotional media in the box.

banners	billboards	brochure	cinema	electric signs
leaflet	magazine	newspaper	pay-per-click advertising	pop-up ads
posters	radio	street furniture	trade press	TV

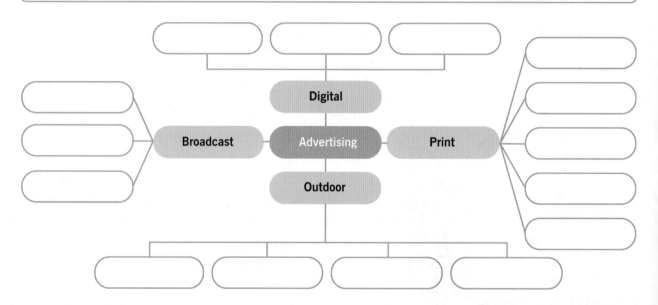

Reading 3

The production of radio and TV commercials can be a big business, almost like making a Hollywood **blockbuster**, with actors, **scriptwriters**, camera operators, producers and directors. Both radio and TV commercials make use of music, whether it is an old or current hit song, something **composed** specifically for the ad or a jingle. Radio obviously does not have the visual impact of TV, so the dialogue becomes even more **fundamental** in getting the message across. Both forms of ads can be conceived as a kind of ongoing story, almost like a soap opera, with new **episodes** every few weeks. Viewers and listeners can become interested in the story and **eagerly** await the next **instalment**, but there is the risk that they miss some of the ads in the **sequence** thus **diminishing** the overall effect and impact.

It is also important to remember that any radio or TV ad must **complement** any existing campaign, for example in print or outdoor, in order to **enhance** and **confirm** the company or brand image.

MY GLOSSARY

blockbuster	*n.*	大片; 畅销书
scriptwriter	*n.*	剧作家; 编剧
compose	*v.*	作曲
fundamental	*adj.*	十分重大的; 根本的
episode	*n.*	（电视连续剧的）一集
eagerly	*adv.*	急切地; 渴望地; 热心地

instalment	*n.*	（报刊上连载小说的）一节
sequence	*n.*	顺序; 一系列
diminish	*v.*	减弱, 缩减
complement	*v.*	补足; 使完美
enhance	*v.*	提高; 增强
confirm	*v.*	证实, 证明; 确认

8 Read the text and answer these questions.

1) What people are involved in making TV and radio commercials?

_____

2) What kind of music can be used?

_____

3) What are the advantages and disadvantages of storyline ads?

_____

4) Why should radio and TV ads be similar in style or content to the rest of a campaign?

_____

9 Match each word to its meaning.

1) blockbuster   a ☐ a person who writes the words for movies or television, etc.

2) scriptwriter   b ☐ something very successful

3) jingle   c ☐ a thin magazine with pictures that gives you information about a product or service

4) fundamental   d ☐ a part or share of a whole

5) downside   e ☐ the disadvantage or less positive aspect of something

6) proportion   f ☐ serious and very important

7) leaflet   g ☐ a little book or a piece of paper containing information about a particular subject

8) brochure   h ☐ a short song used in advertising on radio or television

Listening

10 Listen to this radio commercial and answer these questions.

1) How soon is the name of the company mentioned?

2) What particular service offered by the company is the ad promoting?

3) How does the ad use humour to convey its message?

4) Do you think the ad is successful?

Speaking 2

11 Think of a recent TV commercial and discuss these questions in pairs.

1) What was the ad promoting?

2) Were there famous actors or testimonials?

3) How does it use humour to convey its message?

4) Do you think it is successful?

5) Was it a one-off ad or part of a series or storyline?

6) What music was used?

7) Was it part of a campaign you have also seen in print / online/outdoor or heard on the radio?

8) What is your opinion of the overall ad and its effectiveness?

12 How are these products typically shown in radio and TV commercials in China? How interesting and effective do you find them? How does advertising persuade customers to purchase a particular product? Talk together.

| chocolate bar | trainers | energy drink | smartphone | perfume | car insurance |

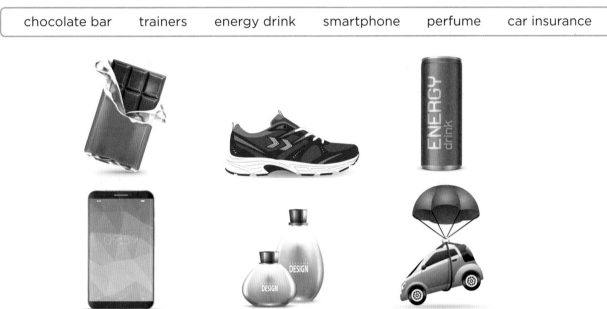

Writing

13 Search online and find some examples of TV ads for the same product but from different periods. Write a short report, describing the features of the ads and saying how they have changed.

Thinking

14 The following text is from CNBC news. Compare online and offline advertising. Which form is more attractive or effective to you? Learn and think.

Half of all global advertising dollars will be spent online by 2020, matching the worldwide combined "offline" ad spend, such as TV, print ads and billboard posters, according to forecasts.

Media agency Magna forecasts that digital media will take 44 percent, or $237 billion, of all ad money spent globally in 2018, with that figure reaching 50 percent, or $291 billion, by 2020.

All forms of digital advertising are on the up, with search advertising the largest segment by far. Marketers are expected to spend $113 billion worldwide next year, a 12 percent increase on 2017. Most of this search ad spend is on mobile, which is due to take 63 percent.

Businesses are expected to spend $147 billion on mobile advertising of all types next year, up 27 percent on 2017. Brands have ever more ways to reach consumers and some are switching most of their ad spend online.

Adidas said it would focus on digital ads over TV, with Chief Executive Kasper Rorsted saying that its younger consumers engaged with the brand mainly via their cellphones.

"All of our engagement with the consumer is through digital media and we believe in the next three years we can take our online business from approximately 1 billion euros ($1.06 billion) to 4 billion euros and create a much more direct engagement with consumers," Chief Executive Kasper Rorsted told CNBC.

Facebook is said to be testing ads that run before video content, possibly part of its strategy to optimise "ad load", or the number of ads on a website or platform. It wants to make sure it has the right balance between "organic" posts—or content from friends—and adverts, Chief Financial Officer Dave Wehner said on a July earnings call.

Useful Expressions and Terms

advertising media 广告媒体

printed advert 印刷广告

visual impact 视觉效果

full colour ad 彩色广告

black and white ad 黑白广告

trade press 行业刊物

specific trades or industries 特定行业

brand awareness 品牌意识

cable TV channels 有线电视频道

on the top three or four networks 排名前三或前四的电视网

prime time slot 黄金时段

skip adverts 跳过广告

take a channel hop 更换频道

purchase the airtime 购买播放时间

the impact of visual images 视觉图像的影响

street furniture 公共设施

more specific market segment 更具体的细分市场

digital media 数字媒体

pop-up ad 弹出广告

pay per click advertising 点击付费广告

create a global community 创建全球化的社区

net surfer 网上冲浪者

millions of hits 数以百万计的点击量

Advertising Standards Authority 广告标准局

regulate all forms of advertising 规范各种形式的广告

tourist attraction 旅游胜地

practical information 实用的信息

opening time 营业时间

hit song 风行一时的歌曲

ongoing story 连续的故事

in the sequence 结果; 后来

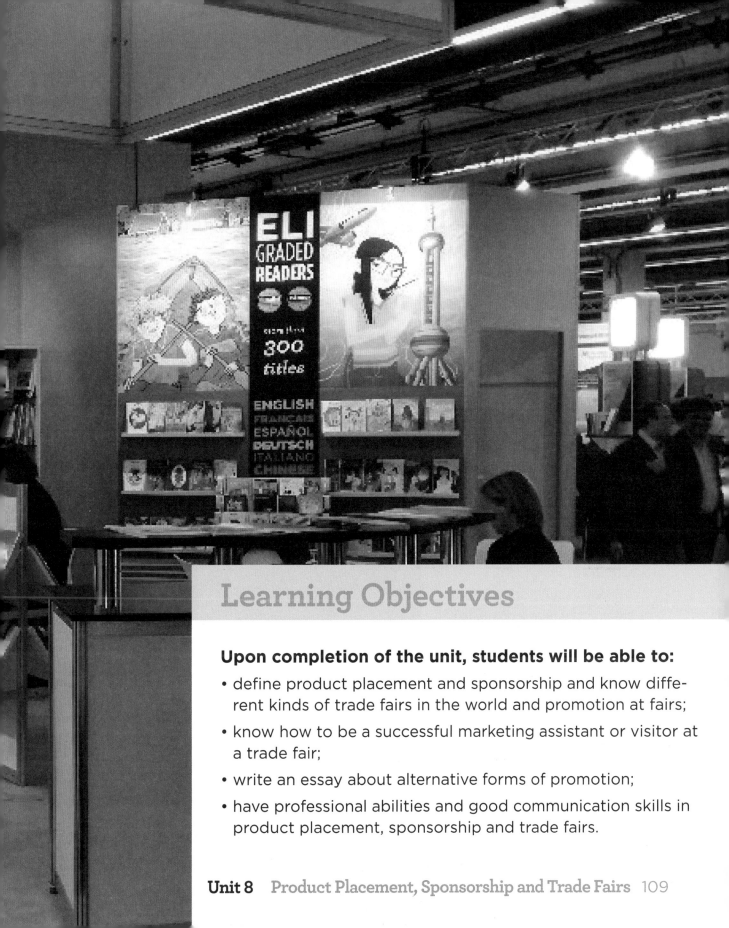

Learning Objectives

Upon completion of the unit, students will be able to:

- define product placement and sponsorship and know different kinds of trade fairs in the world and promotion at fairs;

- know how to be a successful marketing assistant or visitor at a trade fair;

- write an essay about alternative forms of promotion;

- have professional abilities and good communication skills in product placement, sponsorship and trade fairs.

Starting Off

Product placement is a hotly contested form of advertising that can be highly effective when used well. Product placement involves either donating or receiving money in exchange for having your product featured prominently on a television show, movie or even in paparazzi photographs. Sponsorship and trade fairs are both for promoting your products or services. Free-gifting is another way to place a product, but this is hit or miss and relies entirely on famous people actually receiving the item and liking to use it. Let's go on and explore more.

Reading 1

Product Placement

Product **placement** is when a company makes an agreement with the **producers** of a film, music video or TV programme and gives them examples of their products to include in their **production**. It costs a lot of money but can be advantageous for both the advertiser and the production company. The advertiser has the benefit of its product being **associated** with a particular actor in a film, for example, or with a **trendy** TV programme which attracts a huge audience. The film or TV producers can use the money to **finance** their **ventures**. The main disadvantage is probably for the viewer. While a lot of product placement can go almost unnoticed, when it is taken to the extreme and becomes so obvious that it actually interrupts the action or programme, it is as annoying as an actual commercial break. It is in fact due to the worry over **editorial** independence and programmes being **distorted** and becoming **vehicles** for product placement that the practice has only been allowed on British television programmes since 2011.

Sponsorship

Sponsorship is another form of promotion where a company provides money or other kinds of resources to an event, activity or organisation. It is also possible to sponsor TV programmes. This is done by paying a certain amount for a company name to appear in a short **clip** before the programme begins and at the end, rather than for its products to be placed within the programme itself.

For Your Ads Only

Cinema has been using product placement for many years and the 007 movies are no exception. Ever since Sean Connery flew Pan Am and prominently displayed Smirnoff vodka in *Dr. No* fifty years ago, the James Bond movies have slowly but steadily been **invaded** with brands. Bond has been driving Aston Martins since *Goldfinger* (1964), and the occasional BMW too. He crashed through a British Airways billboard in *Moonraker* (1979) and through a Perrier truck in *Goldeneye* (1995). *Skyfall* (2012) prominently featured Heineken beer and the latest movie, *Spectre* (2015), has amongst others N Peal cashmere jumpers and Range Rovers, which raised millions of dollars for the film's budget and shows that there is no end to the companies wanting to include their brands **onscreen**. Brand placement in Bond movies isn't new but, like 007's double entendres, product placement has gotten more shameless.

MY GLOSSARY

placement	*n.*	布置, 放置
producer	*n.*	（电影的）制片人, 制作人
production	*n.*	制作; 生产, 制造
associate	*v.*	联想; 联系
trendy	*adj.*	时髦的, 流行的
finance	*v.*	负担经费; 供给……经费
venture	*n.*	（有风险的）企业; 冒险旅行
editorial	*adj.*	编辑的; 编者的; 主编的
distort	*v.*	扭曲; 曲解
vehicle	*n.*	传播媒介; 手段; 工具
sponsorship	*n.*	赞助; 赞助式广告
clip	*n.*	电影片段
invade	*v.*	侵扰; 涌入; 侵略, 侵袭
onscreen	*adv.*	银幕上

1 Read the text and article and answer these questions.

1) What is product placement?

_____

2) What are the benefits of product placement for the advertiser? And for the production company?

_____

3) Why was it not introduced until 2011 on British TV?

_____

4) What is sponsorship?

_____

5) How does the sponsorship of a TV programme differ from product placement in a TV programme?

_____

6) When did product placement start in Bond films?

_____

7) Which product has been associated with Bond the longest?

_____

8) According to the article, is product placement in Bond films at an extreme level? What do you think?

_____

2 Find synonyms for the following in the text.

1) arrangement   _____

2) beneficial   _____

3) fashionable, popular   _____

4) irritating   _____

5) apprehension, concern _____

6) supplies, goods   _____

3 Complete the conversation about product placement using the expressions in the box.

Hollywood movie	prominent place	more subtle	product placement
around the bush	at the bottom of	hordes of people	slow motion

Victoria: Congratulations are in order. I just scored a(n) (1)_____ for our brand in the latest movie. Thank you, thank you very much.

Gerard: Really? That's great! Will it have a(n) (2)_____ in the movie?

Victoria: Well, you know how these things are. Our logo goes by in the blink of an eye, but millions of people are going to see it.

Gerard: So will the star be wearing our logo on his shirt or something?

Victoria: Something like that.

Gerard: But not that.

Victoria: No, it's a little (3)_____ than that, but it'll be embedded into an important scene.

Gerard: But where are they going to see it?

Victoria: Is that really important? The important thing is that our brand will be associated with a major (4)_____. What more could we ask for?

Gerard: Stop beating (5)_____. Where in the movie will our logo appear?

Victoria: All right. It'll be (6)_____ the star's shoes, on the sole, and the audience will be able to see it when he's running.

Gerard: Only if he's running in (7)_____, but he won't be, right? If it goes by that quickly, it'll be more like subliminal advertising.

Victoria: Exactly! I hadn't thought of it that way, but (8)_____ will be going out to buy our products and they won't even know why. I'm even more of a genius than I thought!

Listening 1

4 **Listen to this explanation of the different kinds of sponsorship and complete these notes.**

Sports sponsorship: Events are seen live and on TV by many people.

Example: (1) _____ in the UK and Europe.

TV and radio sponsorship: (2) _____ channels offer more possibilities.

Example: (3) _____ and dramas.

Arts sponsorship: Considered in line with a company's (4) _____ identity or activity.

Example: shows, exhibitions, concerts.

Educational sponsorship: Sponsor (5) _____ or provide equipment.

Example: Tesco vouchers for sports equipment and (6) _____.

Writing 1

5 **Write a short essay about the forms of promotion, such as product placement and sponsorship according to these questions.**

1) Does product placement in TV programmes exist in your country?

2) If yes, which companies and products are most commonly present?

3) Do you notice when there is product placement in a TV programme or film? How do you feel about it?

4) Is sponsorship more suitable for large or small companies? Why?

5) Do you think sponsorship is a good form of promotion?

Reading 2

Trade Fairs

Participation in **exhibitions** and trade fairs is an important **publicity** measure to promote goods and services on the market. In only 2–4 days at a trade show a company may find more customers, partners and **resellers** than over an entire year of standard methods. Attending trade shows not only helps make **numerous** new contacts but also helps businesses stay updated on industry trends and prepare for the future. Businesses also need to keep an eye on the competition and trade shows are perfect for checking out what competitors are up to.

Some trade fairs are only open to trade visitors, that is companies and professionals in the sector, as well as the press, while others are also open to the general public. The types of

trade fairs cover just about every business sector from **architecture**, **organic** food and green technology to **telecommunications**, IT, and oil and gas. Thanks to all the associated businesses and services such as **accommodation**, food, and stand **construction** or displays, trade fairs **constitute** an important form of income for the cities where major **fairgrounds** are situated.

Major Trade Fair Centres in the World		
Ground	**City**	**Key Trade Fairs**
FieraMilano	Milan	Salone del Mobile, EICMA
Hanover fairground	Hanover	Hannover Messe
Frankfurt Trade Fair	Frankfurt	Frankfurt Book Show, Automechanika
Koelnmesse	Cologne	Gamescom, Art Cologne
Fira de Barcelona	Barcelona	Mobile World Congress
Paris Expo	Paris	Paris Motor Show
Las Vegas Convention Center	Nevada	International Consumer Electronics Show
McCormick Place	Chicago	International Home and Housewares Show, Chicago Auto Show
Tokyo Big Sight	Tokyo	Tokyo Auto Show
China Import and Export Complex	Guangzhou	Canton Fair

participation	*n.*	参与; 参加; 参股		telecommunication	*n.*	电讯; 远程 通信; 电信
exhibition	*n.*	展览会; 展览; 显示				
publicity	*n.*	宣传; 宣扬		accommodation	*n.*	住处; 膳宿
reseller	*n.*	中间商; 转销商		construction	*n.*	建设; 建筑物
numerous	*adj.*	许多的, 很多的		constitute	*v.*	组成, 构成
architecture	*n.*	建筑; 建筑学		fairground	*n.*	商品交易会场址; 展 销会场地
organic	*adj.*	有机的; 绿色的				

6 **Read the text and decide if these sentences below are true (*T*) or false (*F*). If there is not enough information, choose "doesn't say" (*DS*).**

	T	F	DS
1) Trade shows are another form of promotion for a company.	☐	☐	☐
2) Trade shows are particularly useful for the consumer goods industry.	☐	☐	☐
3) They offer the opportunity to see what is happening in a particular sector or industry.	☐	☐	☐
4) Exhibitors can see what their competitors are doing.	☐	☐	☐
5) All trade shows are open to the public.	☐	☐	☐
6) Trade fairs also offer business opportunities to local companies.	☐	☐	☐
7) All big cities in the world have a trade fairground.	☐	☐	☐

7 **Fill in the blanks with the words from the box, changing the form if necessary.**

onscreen	sponsorship	exhibition	telecommunication
vehicle	fairground	constitute	participation

1) The gallery has mounted a(n) _____ of art by Chinese women painters.

2) Two atoms of hydrogen and one of oxygen _____ the water molecule.

3) Business _____ must be a supplement to, not a substitute for, public funding.

4) Because this invention was an American contribution to the World's Fair, it has become a staple of the _____.

5) Such a source can provide important needs, such as lighting, _____ and information transfer.

6) Art may be used as a(n) _____ for propaganda.

7) Many local businesses are _____ in the fundraising event.

8) It was the first movie to feature _____ product placement for its own merchandise.

Speaking 1

8 Go online and find out about a fair or exhibition centre in China. Prepare a short oral presentation about it, including these points:

- the most important exhibitions / trade fairs held
- whether they are open to the public or trade
- the number of visitors
- the facilities available

Writing 2

9 What have you learnt about alternative forms of promotion? Write a short essay (150–200 words) about it following these guidelines:

- product placement and its advantages and disadvantages
- the different types of sponsorship
- the benefits of trade fairs

Promotion at a Fair

If you work for a company that attends fairs and exhibitions, it might be necessary for you to be part of the team on the **stand**, greeting and meeting potential business partners and clients or members of the public. Given the international nature of most fairs, it is likely you will do this in English or another foreign language. Whatever the size of the stand, it needs to have eye-catching displays, such as posters or screens, and promotional material like leaflets, brochures or **gadgets** to hand out.

The people working on the stand need to be friendly and welcoming at all times.

MY GLOSSARY

stand	*n.* （展示或推介物品的）桌, 台, 摊位	gadget	*n.* 小玩意; 小器具

USEFUL LANGUAGE

At a Fair

Open questions
- Which areas are your customers most interested in?
- What's your opinion on the trend for...?
- What type of product is most popular?

Handing out promotional material
- Would you like to take one of our brochures?
- Let me give you a leaflet which explains the...

Taking contact details
- Can I have your / Have you got a business card so I can send you some more details?
- If you fill in this form with your details, we'll enter you into our competition.

10 Translate the following expressions into Chinese.

1) product placement _____

2) the international nature of most fairs _____

3) meet potential business partners _____

4) make an agreement with _____

5) an important publicity measure _____

6) stay updated on industry trends _____

7) in the business sector _____

8) attend fairs and exhibitions _____

11 Reorder the dialogue at a stand at a Food & Beverage trade fair.

☐ **Marketing Assistant:** Well, it depends. Where do you need the coffee machine for?

☐ **Client:** Pods, I think. They're easier, aren't they?

☐ **Marketing Assistant:** And my card. If you leave me your card, I'll contact you to organise demonstration at your company.

☐ **Client:** It's for the reception of our company.

☐ **Marketing Assistant:** Hello. I see you are looking at our coffee machines. Do you prefer one which uses pods or loose beans?

☐ **Client:** That would be perfect. I look forward to your call.

☐ **Marketing Assistant:** I would recommend the FA 20 pod machine then. Here's a leaflet with all the details.

☐ **Client:** Thanks.

Listening 2

12 Listen to two experts talking about how to be successful at a trade show. Decide if the following statements are true (*T*) or false (*F*).

	T	F
1) Stands at trade fairs are often booked up very quickly.	☐	☐
2) The location of your stand within the fair is not important.	☐	☐
3) There is often a financial advantage if you book in advance.	☐	☐
4) The expert advises communicating your presence at the fair only through newsletters to clients.	☐	☐
5) Networking is possibly the most important thing to do at a trade fair.	☐	☐
6) There is no need for specific staff training for a trade fair.	☐	☐

Speaking 2

13 Which of the following things do you think is the most important in a promotional campaign? Why? Discuss with your partner.

- Have a pleasant manner.
- Smile and greet the visitor to the stand warmly.
- Be positive and have an enthusiastic tone of voice to create a rapport.
- Use a mixture of closed questions (for example, "Are you interested in…?") and open questions (for example, "What appeals to you about a…?")
- Listen carefully so you can tailor what you say to the person's needs.
- Be fully knowledgeable about the product/service/destination.
- Where necessary, get contact details, such as a business card, to follow up the potential contact after the event.

14 In pairs, choose one of the options and act out the situation. Then choose another one and swap roles.

Marketing Assistant: You are at a trade fair to promote your company which specialises in restaurant equipment / interior design / office furniture / telecommunications / swimming pools. Talk to the potential client.

Trade Fair Visitor: You are at a trade fair looking for new contacts and suppliers. Talk to the person on the stand to find out more about the company, its products or services.

Thinking

15 The following is about product placement. Are you familiar with it? How does it work? Learn and think.

Product placement creates explicit and implicit advertising effects. Advertisers and producers have become more sophisticated in how they execute product placements. For example, a product's appearance may be relatively overt or seamless. A product avoids showing a label or logo but features a product's distinctive colour or packaging. Product placement is effective because it enables the audience to develop a stronger connection with the brand in a more natural way, rather than being directly marketed to.

Useful Expressions and Terms

product placement 产品植入; 植入式广告

trade fair 贸易展览会

make an agreement with 与……达成协议

give examples of... 举例说明……

be associated with 和……联系在一起

a particular actor 一个特定的演员

trendy TV programme 流行的电视节目

no exception 无一例外

cashmere jumper 羊绒针织衫

brand placement 品牌植入

double entendre 双关语

important publicity measure 重要的宣传措施

on the market 在市场上

at a trade show 在贸易展览会上

standard method 标准方法

make numerous new contacts 结交很多新朋友

stay updated on industry trends 了解最新的行业趋势

keep an eye on 留意; 密切关注

general public 公众, 大众

in the business sector 在商业领域

green technology 绿色技术

stand construction 展台建设

attend fairs and exhibitions 参加交易会和展览会

on the stand 在展台上

meet potential business partners 结识潜在的业务伙伴

UNIT
9 Analysing Adverts

Learning Objectives

Upon completion of the unit, students will be able to:

- understand features of an advert and brand stretching;
- analyse the language, images and other features of adverts and write a slogan and headline for a specific product or service;
- explain the necessities and risks of brand stretching;
- have professional abilities and good communication skills in analysing adverts.

Starting Off

Advertising has become part of our daily life. Most people see and hear a mass of advertising messages every day. An advert is usually composed of a headline, a body copy, a slogan, a logo, a brand name and illustrations. In these elements, headline, body copy and slogan are the most important. A good advert has visual impact, great copy with staying power, perfect placement for the audience, the right timing and the call to action. What elements impressed you the most? Let's go on and explore more.

Reading 1

Features of an Advert

Logo The logo is the immediately **recognisable** and **distinct** symbol which is associated with an organisation or a company. It is used in advertising, but is also seen on the company buildings, vehicles, **stationery** and products.

Brand This is the name that identifies a particular product.

Image This is an extremely powerful element in all types of advertising, except radio which obviously relies on its **auditory** impact. An image is capable of creating a **myriad** of emotions—from making us cry to making us laugh, reflect and remember. Ads often make use of **stereotypes** as a **shorthand** way of communicating a set of meanings and gender stereotypes are perhaps the most common. Men are shown as

practical, wearing **executive** suits and watches, being taller than women and are associated with heavy machinery and business decisions. Women are **decorative**, associated with kitchen equipment, **domestic** financial decisions and are often shown lying down on beds and floors. Given that a lot of our self-identity may **stem** from the images and messages in advertising, stereotyping however can be potentially harmful.

Language Whether it is written or spoken, language is essential to the success of an advert. Top copywriters are well-paid to come up with the next unforgettable slogan, the catchiest headline or persuasive—but not obvious—body copy or dialogue. As advertising is directly addressing a potential customer, one of the most used words is "you". Short, active words have a lot of impact and catch attention and verbs are often in the **imperative** form to encourage action. In outdoor advertising, for example a billboard, it is normal to have only one or two short sentences or slogans as people do not have enough time to stop and read the entire ad as they would with a magazine or a newspaper. **Repetition** helps **reinforce** the message. Other devices, such as **alliteration**, **assonance**, **similes**, **metaphors**, **puns** and word play are also common. However, humour must be used with caution, especially in an international campaign, as what is funny in one country might not be in another. Cultural references and foreign words can also be used, but within a carefully considered demographic target, otherwise the risk is to **alienate** those that do not understand the language or do not have the cultural background to understand the references.

MY GLOSSARY

recognisable	adj.	可辨认的, 可认识的	stem	v.	起源于……
distinct	adj.	明显的, 独特的	imperative	adj.	命令的; 祈使的
stationery	n.	文具; 信纸	repetition	n.	重复; 重复的语句
auditory	adj.	听觉的	reinforce	v.	加强, 加固; 强化
myriad	n.	无数, 极大数量	alliteration	n.	头韵; 头韵法
stereotype	n.	模式化形象, 刻板印象	assonance	n.	类似的音, 谐音; 类韵
shorthand	n.	速记; 速记法	simile	n.	明喻, 直喻
executive	adj.	高级的; 供重要人物使用的	metaphor	n.	暗喻, 隐喻; 比喻说法
decorative	adj.	装饰性的, 装潢用的	pun	n.	双关语; 俏皮话
domestic	adj.	家庭的; 国内的	alienate	v.	使疏远, 离间; 冷落

1 Read the text and use your own words to complete these sentences.

1) A logo differs from a brand because _____.

2) Gender stereotypes are when men are portrayed as _____ and women as _____.

3) Stereotypes may be dangerous because _____.

4) The word "you" is used frequently in advertising because _____.

5) Repetition, alliteration and similes are examples of _____.

6) In advertising, _____ must all be used carefully.

2 Match these functions to the correct description.

| Talking about the emotions | Talking about the features |
| Talking about how an ad persuades | Talking about the target |

1) _____

This kind of ad probably appeals to professional people.

People in the Western world can identify with this ad.

2) _____

It makes you want to become part of a group.

The ad does not actually get the message across very well.

You associate the product with a positive ideal.

It represents a personal ideal or goal and makes it seem obtainable.

3) _____

The font highlights the strong personality of the testimonial.

The colours consist of soft hues which are suitable for the romantic nature of the ad.

It has a bold and aggressive colour scheme which immediately attracts your attention.

The minimal language does not distract from the main message.

4) _____

It creates a feeling of peace and tranquillity.

The atmosphere created is fun and light-hearted.

The mood is quite dark and sombre.

The main image conveys a sense of freedom.

3 Complete the slogans using the words in the box and then match them with the most suitable product/company.

| confident | planet | recharge | ticket | touch |

1) Your _____ to paradise!

    a ☐ an electric car

2) Be _____ and fresh all day long!

    b ☐ a five-star luxury hotel in the Swiss Alps

3) Protect the _____ and your loved ones!

    c ☐ a mobile phone

4) Get away from it all and _____ your batteries!

    d ☐ an airline flying to the Seychelles

5) Keep in _____ wherever you are.

    e ☐ a deodorant

Writing 1

4 Look at these images and write a slogan and headline for a print advert to attract young people to this hotel. Compare your idea with the rest of the class and then vote on the best version.

It is located on a Caribbean island, right on a sandy beach where lots of watersports are available.

There is a tiki bar on the beach, a large infinity pool, with poolside bar, two restaurants and a spa.

Listening

5 **Listen to an expert and a consultant talking about the advantages and disadvantages of advertising and fill in the blanks.**

C: Hello! What on earth is advertising?

E: Well, advertising is a major component of any company's (1)_____. It includes messages that are paid for and delivered to targeted customers via mass media. TV and radio (2)_____, print ads, billboards and a wide array of support media are used to (3)_____. While advertising helps communicate your brand's value, it does have some drawbacks and limitations.

C: What are the advantages and disadvantages of advertising?

E: Advertising messages are largely in the control of the advertiser. When you pay a medium to place your message, you typically (4)_____ over the position, timing and construct of your ad. This allows your business to map out a strategy in advance about how to develop the right messages, and which media best reach the (5)_____.

C: As noted, I have a number of media options in delivering advertising. Any communication channel is a (6)_____. But it is difficult to evaluate the effectiveness of our ads and (7)_____.

E: You can present messages one time, multiple times or tell a long-running story through (8)_____. You can also choose between long-term brand messaging which helps you (9)_____ for your brand, and short-term promotions to attract immediate traffic and sales. Everything depends on you.

C: The disadvantages are?

E: The most obvious drawback of advertising is the (10)_____. Large companies invest millions of dollars a year in advertising. Television ads are very expensive. Production costs range from $100,000 to $500,000 for national ads, and placement can be as much as $500,000 for a 30-second prime-time spot on a national network. Small companies are usually even more limited. Budgets of a few thousand dollars are typical for some local companies.

C: Such are the facts. Thank you very much.

E: You are welcome!

Speaking 1

6 **Look at the pictures on the next page which show common images in advertising and answer these questions. Use these ideas to help you.**

1) What feelings and associations do these images suggest?

- joy
- love
- determination
- family life
- healthy lifestyle

2) What kind of products are they often used to advertise?

- cleaning products
- laundry detergent
- food
- sports clothes
- bottled water
- deodorant

3) Are they effective or too over-used?

4) Do you think using this kind of image promotes stereotypes? Why / Why not?

5) Can using stereotypes in advertising cause offence? Why / Why not?

Reading 2

Brand Stretching

After a brand is well-established and has positive associations and values—such as quality, **innovation** or passion—in the minds of consumers, it is normal for a company to wish to **capitalise** on the brand image and make money by extending an existing brand into new product categories. With their high brand awareness and brand **loyalty**, many luxury labels for example have successfully extended their product lines from clothes to accessories, then stretched them further to perfume, make-up and even to furniture and hotels. However, not all attempts at brand stretching are successful and the risk of damage to the image and **credibility** of the original brand needs to be evaluated. Issues like cost-effective production, distribution and economies of scale all need to be taken into consideration too.

When a company decides it wants to enter in a new area, it is vital to correctly identify the most appropriate product categories. There should be a benefit to the parent brand and the parent brand also needs to give some kind of benefit to the new product. It is also essential to understand what kind of new products consumers will find acceptable. There needs to be a functional fit between the existing brand and the new category of products. This means that consumers can easily relate to the new product and can transfer the values and qualities of the original brand to it. An example is Gillette which moved successfully from razors to **deodorants** and similar products because it already had the credibility in the field of male grooming. Something totally inappropriate would be where consumers can see no connection or correspondence whatsoever between the original brand and the new product, such as a fast-food company launching a skincare product or a **petrochemical** company making ice cream.

Having that said however, research shows that consumers would be willing for some brands to stretch into categories with no functional fit. It depends on the perception of the brand's personality: the warmer and more attractive a brand is, the more **elastic** it seems to be. In these cases, consumers would more easily accept brand stretching into new, unrelated categories.

MY GLOSSARY

innovation	*n.*	创新, 革新; 新方法
capitalise	*v.*	投资于; 用大写字母书写
loyalty	*n.*	忠诚, 忠心, 忠实
credibility	*n.*	可信性; 确实性

deodorant	*n.*	除臭剂; 体香剂
petrochemical	*adj.*	石油化工的; 石油化学的
elastic	*adj.*	灵活的; 有弹性的

7 **Match each phrase with the correct definition.**

1) brand awareness   **a** ☐ using an established brand name in a different product category

2) brand loyalty   **b** ☐ the extent to which the existence of a brand is recognised by potential consumers

3) brand stretching

4) brand recall   **c** ☐ the ability of a consumer to remember a particular brand when the product is mentioned

   d ☐ how consistently a consumer purchases the same brand within a product category

8 **Read the text again and decide if these sentences are true (*T*) or false (*F*). If there is not enough information, choose "doesn't say" (*DS*).**

	T	F	DS
1) Brand stretching is a way for a company to make more money.	☐	☐	☐
2) Luxury designers have been successful in stretching their brands.	☐	☐	☐
3) Brand stretching cannot harm the image of the original brand.	☐	☐	☐
4) There should be reciprocal benefits for the original brand and new product.	☐	☐	☐
5) Consumers should be consulted before making a decision on brand stretching.	☐	☐	☐
6) For brand stretching to be effective, there should be a connection between the original brand and new product.	☐	☐	☐

7) Fast-food companies cannot successfully stretch their brands. ☐ ☐ ☐

8) Consumers would never accept a brand if it stretched into an unconnected category. ☐ ☐ ☐

9 Translate the following expressions into Chinese.

1) analysing adverts   _____

2) features of an advert   _____

3) the recognisable and distinct symbol   _____

4) auditory impact   _____

5) gender stereotypes   _____

6) business decisions   _____

7) word play   _____

8) economies of scale   _____

9) the perception of the brand's personality   _____

10) brand stretching   _____

10 Fill in the blanks with words from the box, changing the form if necessary.

repetition	credibility	reinforce	decorative	distinct
innovation	executive	stereotype	imperative	domestic

1) The most important political _____ thing is to limit the number of US casualties.

2) We must promote originality, inspire creativity and encourage _____.

3) He entered the building with a(n) _____ briefcase in his hand.

4) The snow leopard is a species that is _____ from the leopard species.

5) _____ duties and activities are concerned with the running of a home and family.

6) Adverts can effectively persuade customers through _____.

7) The team captain was failing in school, and he was sadly convinced that he fitted the _____ of the dimwitted athlete.

8) The teacher allowed him to make up the exam because she thought his excuse was _____.

9) The curtains are purely for _____ purposes and do not open or close.

10) Remember you want your visuals to _____ your message, not detract from what you are saying.

Speaking 2

11 **Answer these questions in pairs.**

1) What examples of brand stretching can you think of?

2) Are you loyal to a particular brand? Think about toiletries and beauty, clothes, technology, cars.

3) Would you consider buying a new product just because of the brand?

12 **Think of a recent print or TV ad and describe it to your partner. You can talk about the images, atmosphere, type of language and other features and you can mention the type of product or service being advertised but do not mention the brand or company name. How long does it take for your partner to guess the advert?**

Writing 2

13 **Find an advert that you particularly like and print / cut out a copy. Write a short analysis of the features of the advert, saying why you like it and what makes it effective.**

Thinking

14 **The following is a mobile ad. Do you think it is ultra-concise and fast? How about the call to action in the mobile ad? Learn and think.**

Mobile ad space is limited. Shopify was able to do that in the Facebook ad that popped up in our mobile newsfeed: We'd almost be surprised if this wasn't a mobile-only ad. "Sell Your Crafts on FB!" and "Sell online, in-store, and on Facebook…" are both incredibly brief, which works as a strong advantage on this platform where brevity is key. The ellipsis following Facebook that leads right into the "Learn More" button is also a smart move, taking us from one thought right to the clickable CTA button.

Useful Expressions and Terms

the recognisable and distinct symbol 易于识别的独特标志

auditory impact 听觉效果

create a myriad of emotions 引发各种情感

gender stereotype 性别刻板印象

executive suit 高级套装

kitchen equipment 厨房设备

domestic financial decision 家庭财务的决断

reinforce the message 强化信息

word play 文字游戏

in the minds of customers 在客户心目中

brand image 品牌形象

brand loyalty 品牌忠实度

luxury label 奢侈品牌

extend product line 扩大产品线

brand stretching 品牌扩张

original brand 原始品牌

economies of scale 规模经济

product category 产品类别

parent brand 母品牌

a functional fit 功能性的契合

in the field of male grooming 男性美容领域

launch a skincare product 推出一款护肤品

petrochemical company 石油化工企业

perception of the brand's personality 感知品牌特色

Learning Objectives

Upon completion of the unit, students will be able to:

- understand the key features of a CV and the Europass CV, tips for a successful interview and different jobs in the advertising industry;

- write a CV and a covering letter and successfully prepare a job interview;

- have professional abilities and good communication skills in job hunting.

Starting Off

If you are a job seeker, "You're hired!" are the words you love to hear. But when you are finding a job, writing a CV or a covering letter isn't enough. What you still have to do is to survive the interview in order to get the job offer. It's important that you prepare everything. First, study yourself and find out what job you really want. Second, research the company you are interested in and find out the available position. The last but not least, you must treat looking for a job like a job itself, and thus you will find a job much sooner. Let's go on and explore more.

Reading 1

Curriculum Vitae (CV)

How to Write a CV

A **curriculum vitae**, CV for short, is a brief summary of facts about you and your qualifications, work history, skills and experience. It is essential to have a good CV when applying for a job as it is your chance to sell yourself and be selected for an interview. Some companies may ask you to fill in an application form instead of sending a CV.

Your CV should be:

- printed on white paper and no more than 2 or 3 sides;

- clear and correct;

- positive and make a good impression, emphasising your strengths and skills;

- adapted to suit the specific job profile.

Key Features

Personal details
Your name, address, phone number(s), email address and date of birth.

Personal profile
This is normally at the beginning of the CV. It is a short statement aimed at selling yourself so you should use positive words and expressions. It must be specifically written for the position you are applying for.

Work experience
It is normal practice to list your most recent job first, with the dates. It is not a good idea to leave any gaps between dates and if you do not have a lot of experience, you should include details of part-time and voluntary work.

Qualifications and training
This includes qualifications from school and university as well as any other training courses or **certificates**. You should indicate the date (the most recent first), the title of the qualification, the level obtained and the organisation/place.

Achievements/Skills/Competences
This can include foreign languages and computer skills, as well as things like artistic or musical skills. It is possible to highlight a particular achievement—personal or professional—which **reflects** well on your ability to do the job.

Interests
Hobbies or sports activities can help show particular abilities or skills which could be relevant for the job.

References
This section is for the name, position and contact details of at least two people who can provide a personal and/or work reference. Alternatively it is possible to state that references can be supplied on request.

curriculum vitae		简历
competence	*n.*	技能; 本领
reflect	*v.*	反映; 表达; 显示

reference	*n.*	推荐人; 介绍人; 介绍信
certificate	*n.*	文凭; 结业证书; 合格证书

1 Read the text and answer these questions.

1) What is the purpose of a CV?

2) How long should it be? Why do you think that is?

3) Is it a good idea to use the same CV for different job applications? Why / Why not?

4) Why do you think the personal profile is normally at the start of the CV?

5) What order should you list your qualifications and previous jobs? Why do you think that is?

6) What kind of interests do you think would be positive to include in your CV?

7) What is the purpose of indicating references?

8) Can you think of examples of positive words and expressions for a CV?

2 Discuss these questions according to the CV and the job advertisement.

Jeremy Keystone JK

Address	7 High Street, Rochford, SS4 7PT
Phone	01702 986631
Email	jeremy.keystone@virgin.net

Personal profile

I am highly motivated and work well as part of a team. My overseas professional experience at The Silver Ivy — Hotel and Conference Centre, Gibraltar as Security Supervisor taught me to adapt to new situations and to work under challenging conditions and high standard levels. I am now looking for a position as a Security Manager to develop my career and duties.

Qualifications

2009 – 2012   Associates degree in Criminal Justice
Manchester University

2006 – 2008   Certification in Security Management
Hope Sixth Form College, Luton

Work history

November 2012   Security Supervisor at The Silver Ivy — Hotel and Conference Centre, Gibraltar

Sept. 2008 – June 2009   Deputy Security Supervisor at Johnson's Hall Conference Centre, Leeds

Interests   I enjoy scuba diving and water sports. I started sports as a team player with basketball.

References   Dr Craig Knowles
Hotel Manager at The Silver Ivy — Hotel and Conference Centre, Gibraltar

Ms Susan Knight
General Manager Johnson's Hall Conference Centre, Leeds

1) Does the CV follow all the advice given in Reading 1?

2) Is the candidate fit for the job?

3) What position is being advertised?

4) What requisites are they looking for?

5) Does the candidate have the right experience and qualifications?

6) Does the CV make a positive impression? Why / Why not?

Security Job Post—The Guardian GUARD

Job Summary

Company
Celtic Security Ltd.

Location
London, UK

Job Type
● Full Time

Smithson's Medical Group—Director of Security

Job Responsibilities/Duties
- Plans and organizes the day-to-day operation of the Security Department
- Assures the Clinic is in compliance with regulatory agency requirements.
- Plans and schedules fire, safety, and code pink drills.
- Coordinates parking arrangements for all departments and employees.
- Supervises all employees in the Security Department.
- Works in conjunction with Bio-med and Engineering regarding HIPAA security requirements.

Qualifications
Minimum Education: High School diploma or equivalent.
Minimum Experience: Ten (10) years' experience in Security and five (5) years of supervisory experience required. Hospital security experience preferred.

3 **Have you ever seen a Europass CV? How do you think it differs from a standard CV? Talk together.**

The Europass CV is a standard document aimed at simplifying the job application process between EU member states for both employers and applicants. It is possible to complete the CV online or to download it, together with examples and instructions on how to fill it in.

There are five Europass documents designed to make your skills and qualifications clearly and easily understood in Europe. In addition to the CV, there is the European Skills Passport, which includes a Language Passport, Europass Mobility, Certificate Supplement and Diploma Supplement.

The European Skills passport can be attached to the Europass CV to give comprehensive details of your skills and qualifications, grouping together copies of certificates and degrees and proof of employment.

Europass also offers the possibility to compile covering letters and gives suggestions for key expressions for each part.

euro**pass**

Europass Curriculum Vitae

Personal information

First name(s)/Surname(s)	**Sabina Cerratani**
Address	Via Monte Bianco 428, 20131 Milan (Italy)
Mobile	330 9000012345
Email(s)	sabi_cerra@gmail.com
Nationality	Italian
Date of birth	02/09/1995
Gender	Female

Desired employment/ Occupational field	**Publishing and translating**

Work experience

Dates	12/2014 →
Occupation or position held	Editorial Assistant
Main activities and responsibilities	Translation of correspondence into English and Spanish Assisting at international book fairs
Name and address of employer	GFR SpA Via Torino, 20123 Milan (Italy)
Type of business or sector	Publishing

Education and training

Dates	2010/2014
Title of qualification awarded	Italian High School Certificate
Name and type of organisation providing education and training	IISS Pietro Vieri (Business High School) Via Lattanzio, Milano (Italy)

Personal skills and competences

Mother tongue(s)	**Italian**

Other language(s)

Self-assessment	Understanding				Speaking				Writing	
European level (*)	Listening		Reading		Spoken interaction		Spoken production			
English	C1	Proficient user	C1	Proficient user	C1	Proficient user	C1	Proficient user	C1	Proficient user
Spanish	B2	Independent user	B2	Independent user	C1	Proficient user	C1	Proficient user	B2	Independent user

(*) Common European Framework of Reference (CEF) level

Social skills and competences	Ability to adapt to multicultural environments, thanks to extensive travel
Organisational skills and competences	Excellent coordination skills developed during 2 years as Editor of school newspaper
Computer skills and competences	Microsoft Office
Artistic skills and competences	Sculpture
Other skills and competences	Interested in travel, world food, cinema
Driving licence(s)	B
Additional information	Reference: Mr P. Sagripanti, Principal, IIIS Pietro Verri, Milan

How to Write a Covering Letter

Jeremy Keystone
7 High Street
Rochford
SS4 7PT
Tel: 01702 986631
jeremy.keystone@virgin.net

Ms Lewis Carol,
Celtic Security Ltd.,
83 Wimbledon Park Side, London
SW19 5LP

17th April 20..

Dear Ms Lewis,

> Here you should refer to the advertisement and where you saw it. Include the title of the position and any reference number.

I am writing in response to your advertisement in *The Guardian* and wish to apply for the post of Director of Security.

> Here you can give a few details about your qualifications and/or experience.

After training school, where I gained knowledge and related skills in carrying out security operations and **procedures** in accordance to **prescribed** rules and regulations, I started working as Deputy Security **Supervisor**, then I attended Manchester University to deepen my knowledge in Security. Since graduation I have been working as Security Supervisor at a five star **superior** hotel. My strengths can be summed up as follows:

- Extensive experience in handling general security operations including facility **inspection**, updating of paper work and security **manuals**;
- Demonstrated ability to command and control FCC activities during emergency situations;
- Well **versed** in reviewing and investigating accidental and **misconduct** reports and issuing future course of action in light of **incident** analysis;
- Able to assess staff and **personnel** training needs and provide training accordingly.

> This is your chance to state why you would be perfect for the company. Do not just use the same letter for every job application. Each letter should be **tailored** to the specific **requisites** mentioned in the ad.

Having worked for two international security groups, my skills in security management have been **refined** by experience. With a 10+ years' career in the security field, I feel confident that I can contribute significantly to the role of Director of Security at Smithson's Medical Group.

> Here you can mention any **enclosures** (CV, references, certificates) and state how you are going to follow up on your letter.

Please find enclosed my Curriculum Vitae and I would welcome the opportunity to provide further information during an interview.

I look forward to hearing from you.

Yours sincerely,
Jeremy Keystone
Jeremy Keystone

Enc.

procedure	n.	程序; 手续; 步骤
prescribe	v.	规定; 命令; 指示
supervisor	n.	监督人; 指导者; 主管人
superior	adj.	质量卓越的; 出类拔萃的
inspection	n.	检查; 查看
manual	n.	使用手册; 指南
versed	adj.	精通的; 熟练的

misconduct	n.	失职; 处理不当
incident	n.	事件, 事故
personnel	adj.	有关人事的
refine	v.	改进; 改善; 使精练
tailor	v.	专门制作; 定做
requisite	n.	必需的事物
enclosure	n.	（信中）附件

4 Read the text and answer the questions below.

1) Why is a covering letter important?

_____

2) How should a covering letter be written?

_____

3) How does a covering letter usually start?

_____

4) Should a covering letter repeat all the details of a CV? Why / Why not?

_____

5) Why is it not a good idea to use a standard covering letter for all applications?

_____

Writing

5 Complete the following covering letter with the missing information in the box, changing the form if necessary.

gained knowledge and related skills	in response to your advertisement
I'm well-organised	apply for the post of Account Manager
please find enclosed	I have 10 years' experience in the same role
so I would be available for an interview	managing the project

Dear Ms Sampson Quain,

    I am writing (1)_____ in *The Guardian* and wish to (2)_____.

In university, I (3)_____ in solving problems and written and oral communication. Since graduation I have been working in the advertising industry, so I have a good understanding of all the advertising businesses. (4)_____. My skills have been refined by experience. I can speak English and Chinese. (5)_____ _____, with strong attention to detail. I have extensive experience in giving briefings to the creative and strategic teams and (6) _____. I feel confident that I can contribute significantly to the role of Account Manager.

(7)_____ my Curriculum Vitae and I will be in London in two weeks, (8) _____. I am available in 1 month starting from today.

I'm looking forward to hearing from you.

Yours sincerely

Alison Green

Reading 3

Tips for a Successful Interview

Job interviews can be stressful; however, with the proper planning and preparation, you can get the job. Read these tips to help you **survive** the interview and get the job offer.

Before the Interview

- Research the company and prepare relevant questions. Interviewers **appreciate** when job candidates show interest in the company and available position.

- Organise all **paperwork**, including your CV and **eventual** references from previous employers.

- Plan **responses** to common interview questions and practise interviewing with a **peer**.

- Prepare for questions about salary expectations by finding out how much employees in the position you are applying for are **typically** paid.

During the Interview

- Make a good first impression by arriving on time for the interview. Make sure to dress in clean and professional **attire**. Finally, be polite and use the interviewer's name when speaking.

- Respond to all questions clearly. Interviewees should provide **solid** examples of how their previous experience relates to skills needed for the new position. Also be sure to explain your future career goals.

After the Interview

- Employers may request a call-back to obtain more information as a follow-up.

survive	v.	艰难度过; 幸存
appreciate	v.	欣赏, 赏识; 重视
paperwork	n.	全部资料; 文书工作
eventual	adj.	最后的, 最终的
response	n.	反应; 响应

peer	n.	同等地位的人; 同龄人
typically	adv.	通常; 一般
attire	n.	服装; 衣服
solid	adj.	可靠的; 可信赖的

6 Read the text and decide if these sentences are true (*T*) or false (*F*). Then correct the false ones.

	T	F
1) A job candidate should ask about the company during the interview.	☐	☐
2) Interviewees make a good impression by dressing professionally for the interview.	☐	☐
3) A call-back is a typical way for a job candidate to follow up after an interview.	☐	☐
4) Talking about career goals and salary is not recommended.	☐	☐
5) Prepare your CV and references before the interview.	☐	☐
6) Before the interview find out about the company via the Web.	☐	☐

Speaking 2

7 Which of the points in Reading 3 do you think are the most important? Why? Can you think of any other Dos and Don'ts for an interview?

Listening

8 Listen to the job interview between Smith and Tom Kelly and fill in the blanks.

K: Hello Ms Smith, I'm Tom Kelly. Thanks so much for coming.

S: It's my pleasure, thanks so much for meeting with me.

K: Of course. Did you have any trouble finding the office?

S: No. The directions (1)_____ were great.

K: Good. Would you like some coffee or water before we begin?

S: I'm OK, thank you.

K: Alright. So, (2)_____, why don't you tell me a little bit about yourself?

S: Sure. I studied at the University of Florida and graduated in 2010 with a (3)_____ in advertising. After graduation, I was hired at an advertising agency. I've been there for the past 10 years and I am currently (4)_____, but I have no room to grow. I have a lot of experience leading teams in the creative process and finding new clients.

K: That's great. What is your greatest strength?

S: While I'm good with facts and figures, my greatest strength is in communication, (5)_____ _____.

K: Do you have any weaknesses?

S: Maybe one thing I should mention is that I'm a (6)_____ person and tend to overdo things, but I'm still able to manage my time well and (7)_____.

K: What are your goals for the next 5 years?

S: I hope that I can (8)_____ in the management position.

K: …

9 **Listen to the job interview again and answer these questions.**

1) Why does Tom Kelly ask questions like "Did you have any trouble finding the office?" and "Would you like some coffee or water before we begin?"

_____

2) What are the common questions in a job interview?

_____

3) Where does Ms Smith get the information of the job interview?

_____

4) What position does she apply for?

_____

5) Is she qualified for the position?

_____

Speaking 3

10 How many different jobs can you think of in the advertising industry? Do you think advertising would be an interesting field to work in? What opportunities are there in advertising in your area/country? Talk together.

Reading 4

Advertising is a fast-moving and competitive industry. To get a job in this field, you need to be extremely determined, taking advantage of any opportunity of work experience and **internship** to get you ahead of the others. You must also be prepared to start at the bottom.

Here are the profiles of three jobs which can be found in an integrated agency (one which offers all services), in a creative agency and in a media agency.

Account Manager

The main role of an account manager is to act as a **liaison** between the client and the agency. He or she has to meet with the clients to understand their needs, keep them **updated** on what is happening in the projects and solve any problems. An Account Manager works with all the departments within the agency, giving **briefings** to the creative and **strategic** teams, managing the project and ensuring **deadlines** are met and budgets are respected. An Account  Manager should have a good understanding of all the advertising business. He or she needs to be **people-oriented**, sociable, with strong written and oral communication skills in order to **convey** information clearly and convince clients. Other personal qualities include being well-organised, good at solving problems and **flexibility**. The work is very fast-paced and varied. Although often quite well-paid, an Account Manager is expected to work well under pressure and respect strict deadlines, with little regard to traditional working hours. There may be a lack of job security if the agency loses major clients and business.

Media Planner/Buyer

A Media Planner is the person responsible for deciding which media to use in a campaign in order to communicate effectively with the client's target audience. A Media Buyer **negotiates** with media owners to get the best possible rate and space/airtime/position. Sometimes these two roles can be covered by a single person. Media planning involves having an in-depth knowledge of the media (whether it is TV, print or digital media) and then analysing the data and statistics in order to select the

best ones for a successful campaign. It is also important to keep up-to-date with developments in the industry and competitors' strategies. As well as negotiating rates, a Media Buyer has to manage the media bookings, prepare cost reports and analyse the effectiveness of the advertising campaign. The two teams must **coordinate** with each other to ensure the campaign runs on time and to budget. Both Media Planners and Buyers need to work well as part of a team, have good IT skills and be confident at dealing with data and statistics. They should be well-organised, with strong attention to detail.

Copywriter

A Copywriter is the creative mind who writes copy, that is the words that will be used in any form of advertising or marketing, from the slogan for a print ad or the script for a TV ad to a page on a website or company brochure. Copywriters can work for agencies, as well as in house in private and public sector companies. After a briefing to discuss the client's needs, target audience and the advertising strategy to be **adopted**, a Copywriter often works together with an Art Director to create an idea

that will be attractive to the target audience while at the same time satisfying the various client demands. A Copywriter needs to be imaginative and creative, with lots of new ideas and the ability to think outside the box. The work environment is often quite informal but the hours can be long and there is a lot of pressure to complete work within the given deadline. It offers a lot of job satisfaction, but a Copywriter must also be able to accept **criticism** and **rejection** of his/her work.

MY GLOSSARY

internship	n.	实习期; 实习工作; 实习机会
liaison	n.	联络员; 联系
update	v.	向……提供最新信息; 更新
briefing	n.	信息发布会; 情况介绍会
strategic	adj.	战略性的; 战略上的
deadline	n.	最后期限; 截止日期
people-oriented	adj.	以人为本的
convey	v.	表达, 传递（思想、感情等）
flexibility	n.	灵活性; 弹性
negotiate	v.	磋商; 商定; 达成（协议）
coordinate	v.	使协调; 使相配合
adopt	v.	采用（某方法）; 采取（某态度）
criticism	n.	批评; 指责
rejection	n.	拒绝; 抛弃; 被抛弃的东西

11 Read the three job descriptions and complete the table for each one.

Job Title	Role	Description of Tasks	Personal Qualities & Skills
Account Manager	to liaise between client and agency		

12 Complete the table by putting the correct noun, verb or adjective.

Noun	Verb	Adjective
advertisement/advertising		–
	analyse	analytical
attraction	attract	
competition		
creation		
		descriptive
		developed/developing
identification		identifiable
		illustrative/illustrated
		informative
personalisation		
persuasion		promotional
		satisfactory/satisfied

13 Complete these sentences with the correct form of the words in brackets.

1) The _____ of market research data is important to help develop an effective marketing strategy. (analyse)

2) A _____ text usually contains adjectives and appealing expressions. (description)

3) The brochure doesn't contain many _____ or photos, so it isn't very interesting. (illustrate)

4) In a SWOT analysis, strengths are resources and capabilities that can be used to develop a _____ advantage. (competition)

5) Holiday companies often use _____ people to advertise their products. (attract)

6) Well-made _____ are crucial to the success of a TV or press campaign. (advertise)

7) The research and _____ of products is carried out by the R&D department in a company. (develop)

8) Leaflets, brochures and circular letters are forms of _____ material. (promotion)

14 Combine the words from each column to form common collocations.

1) market	a ☐ friendly
2) SWOT	b ☐ audience
3) advertising	c ☐ identity
4) target	d ☐ research
5) brand	e ☐ campaign
6) user	f ☐ analysis

15 **The following job advertisement is from a portal website. What do you think about it? Learn and think.**

A job advertisement is an online, print media or televised announcement of an open position. Depending on the job requirements—and the company's size—the owner may write the ad himself, or refer it to the human resources department. Effective job ads indicate the kind of role a successful applicant will play after he's hired, and the company's expectations for his performance. Because of the large number of candidates applying for jobs daily, hiring a quality employee for a position can be a difficult task.

Interactive Job portal website & mobile apps version

Skills: Website Design, PHP, HTML, Android, Mobile App Development

See more: build job portal website, designing job portal website, project job portal website design html, job portal website project, additional feature needed job portal website, create naukri com type job portal website, features job portal website, free job portal website joomla, give strings dice job portal website, job portal website creator, job portal website design sample, job portal website header banner, job portal website icons buttons, job portal website xml, module list job portal website, sample quotation job portal website, job portal website required, power point presentation job portal website, feature job portal website, presentation job portal website

About the Employer:

5.0 ★★★★★ (2 reviews)   KAJANG, Malaysia

Project ID: #28841010

Offer to work on this job now! Bidding closes in 6 days

OPEN - 6 DAYS LEFT

Your bid for this job

Your Bid	USD

Your email address

Email Address

Bid on this job

✓ Set your budget and timeframe
✓ Outline your proposal

✓ Get paid for your work
✓ It's free to sign up and bid on jobs

Useful Expressions and Terms

for short 缩写; 简言之

application form 申请表

emphasise one's strengths and skills 强调自己的优势和技能

personal profile 个人简历

the title of the qualification 证书名称

associate degree 大专文凭

Deputy Security Supervisor 安保副主管

job responsibilities/duties 岗位职责

security experience preferred 有安保经验者优先

simplify the job application process 简化工作申请流程

covering letter 求职信; 附信

Director of Security 安保负责人

prescribed rules and regulations 指定的规章制度

extensive experience 丰富的经验

be well versed in 精通; 了解

course of action 行动方案

in light of incident analysis 根据事件分析

please find enclosed 随信附上

get the job offer 得到这份工作

salary expectation 期望的薪水

in clean and professional attire 穿着整洁的职业装

advertising industry 广告业

start at the bottom 从基层做起

job profile 工作简介

integrated agency 综合性机构

Account Manager 客户经理

convey information clearly 清晰地传达信息

convince clients 说服客户

personal qualities 个人素质

respect strict deadline 严格遵守最后的期限

lack of job security 缺乏工作保障

Media Planner 媒体策划者

an in-depth knowledge of 对……的深入了解

data and statistics 数据统计

manage the media bookings 管理媒体预定

strong attention to detail 注重细节

job satisfaction 工作满意度